JESUS AND THE EMPIRE OF GOD

CASCADE COMPANIONS

The Christian theological tradition provides an embarrassment of riches: from Scripture to modern scholarship, we are blessed with a vast and complex theological inheritance. And yet this feast of traditional riches is too frequently inaccessible to the general reader.

The Cascade Companions series addresses the challenge by publishing books that combine academic rigor with broad appeal and readability. They aim to introduce nonspecialist readers to that vital storehouse of authors, documents, themes, histories, arguments, and movements that comprise this heritage with brief yet compelling volumes.

SOME OTHER TITLES IN THIS SERIES:

The Canaanites by Mary Ellen Buck
Deuteronomy by Jack Lundbom
David: A Man after God's Own Heart by Benjamin J. M. Johnson
Jeremiah: Prophet Like Moses by Jack Lundbom
Approaching Job by Andrew Zak Lewis
Reading John by Christopher W. Skinner
Reading Acts by Joshua Jipp
Reading Paul by Michael Gorman
Reading 1 Corinthians by J. Brian Tucker
The Letter to the Hebrews in Social-Scientific Perspective by David A. deSilva
Reading Philippians by Nijay K. Gupta
A Companion to Philemon by Lewis Brogdon
Conflict, Community, and Honor: 1 Peter in Social-Scientific Perspective by John H. Elliott
A Companion to the Book of Revelation by David L. Mathewson
Scripture's Knowing: A Companion to Biblical Epistemology by Dru Johnson
Theological Interpretation of Scripture by Stephen E. Fowl
The Second-Century Apologists by Alvyn Pettersen
The Rule of Faith: A Guide by Everett Ferguson
Origen by Ronald E. Heine

JESUS AND THE EMPIRE OF GOD

Reading the Gospels in the Roman Empire

WARREN CARTER

CASCADE *Books* • Eugene, Oregon

JESUS AND THE EMPIRE OF GOD
Reading the Gospels in the Roman Empire

Cascade Companions

Copyright © 2021 Warren Carter. All rights reserved. Except for brief quotations in critical publications or reviews, no part of this book may be reproduced in any manner without prior written permission from the publisher. Write: Permissions, Wipf and Stock Publishers, 199 W. 8th Ave., Suite 3, Eugene, OR 97401.

Cascade Books
An Imprint of Wipf and Stock Publishers
199 W. 8th Ave., Suite 3
Eugene, OR 97401

www.wipfandstock.com

PAPERBACK ISBN: 978-1-7252-9460-8
HARDCOVER ISBN: 978-1-7252-9461-5
EBOOK ISBN: 978-1-7252-9462-2

Cataloguing-in-Publication data:

Names: Carter, Warren, 1955–, author.

Title: Jesus and the empire of God : reading the Gospels in the Roman Empire / Warren Carter.

Description: Eugene, OR: Cascade Books, 2021 | Series: Cascade Companions | Includes bibliographical references.

Identifiers: ISBN 978-1-7252-9460-8 (paperback) | ISBN 978-1-7252-9461-5 (hardcover) | ISBN 978-1-7252-9462-2 (ebook)

Subjects: LCSH: Bible—Gospels—Criticism, interpretation, etc. | Rome in the Bible | Rome—In the Bible | Opposition (Political science) in the Bible | Jesus Christ—Political and social views

Classification: BS2555.2 C37 2021 (paperback) | BS2555.2 (ebook)

06/01/21

The image of the Monument of Philopappos in chapter 3 is licensed under the Creative Commons Attribution-Share Alike 3.0 Unported license. Permission is granted to copy, distribute and/or modify this document under the terms of the GNU Free Documentation License, Version 1.2 or any later version. Attribution: I, Calidius.

CONTENTS

Abbreviations • vii

1 Gospel Texts Are Not Islands: Cultural Intertextuality • 1

2 Gospels and Ancient Biographies • 20

3 Origins • 39

4 Portents of Greatness • 61

5 Jesus: Teacher of Societal Structures and Practices • 82

6 Miracles, Signs, and Wonders • 101

7 Jesus Enters Jerusalem • 123

8 Jesus Dies • 148

9 Jesus' Resurrection, Ascension, Return • 173

10 Conclusion • 195

Bibliography • 197

ABBREVIATIONS

All citations of classical texts are from Loeb Classical Library editions unless otherwise indicated.

Ann   Tacitus, *Annals*

Ant   Josephus, *Antiquities of the Jews*

Hist Tacitus, *Histories*

JW   Josephus, *Jewish War*

NH   Pliny, *Natural History*

Sat   Juvenal, *Satires*

All biblical citations are taken from the New Revised Standard Version unless otherwise specified as "author's translation."

1

GOSPEL TEXTS ARE NOT ISLANDS
Cultural Intertextuality

THE NEW TESTAMENT AND THE ROMAN EMPIRE

THE NEW TESTAMENT GOSPELS come into existence in a world under the rule of the Roman Empire. Though written in the last decades of the first century, the Gospels set their narratives in the beginning of the first century in Galilee-Judea in the rule of Herod and thereafter in the rule of the Emperor Tiberius who died in the year 37 CE and in the governorship of Pontius Pilate (26–37 CE):

> In the fifteenth year of the reign of Emperor Tiberius, when Pontius Pilate was governor of Judea, and Herod was ruler of Galilee, and his brother Philip ruler of the region of Ituraea and Trachonitis, and Lysanias ruler of Abilene, during the high priesthood of Annas and Caiaphas,

> the word of God came to John son of Zechariah
> in the wilderness. (Luke 3:1–2)

The main character, Jesus, was born when the Rome-appointed client king Herod was king of Judea.

> In the time of King Herod, after Jesus was born
> in Bethlehem of Judea, wise men from the East
> came to Jerusalem, asking, "Where is the child
> who has been born king of the Jews?" (Matt
> 2:1–2)

The designation "king of the Jews" puts Jesus off-side with Roman rule since only Rome-appointed figures could legitimately claim to be kings. Kingly figures not sanctioned by Rome were executed. Jesus conducts most of his activity in Rome-ruled Galilee. Adding to tense interaction with Roman power is his central proclamation that "the kingdom/empire of God has come near" (Mark 1:15). The language of "kingdom/empire" both replicates the language of the Roman Empire as well as contests it by asserting another empire in its midst. Jesus moves to Jerusalem, where the Roman governor Pilate executes him by crucifixion.

These are just a few of the obvious points of contact between the Gospels and the Roman Empire. Many more will emerge in the following chapters as we identify further interactions—at times imitative, at times conflictual, at times reinscribing—between the Gospels and Rome's empire. The empire does not disappear from the Gospels just because an emperor or governor or soldier or tax is not mentioned. Rome-sanctioned, Jerusalem-based local leaders, pervasive sickness, food insecurity, occupied territory, language of sovereignty, fantasies of revenge, and visions of a new and just world all interact with Roman imperial structures and practices.

Gospel Texts Are Not Islands

CULTURAL INTERTEXTUALITY

This approach is called cultural intertextuality.[1] It represents an approach that places texts into relationship with other texts to create meaning. It does not claim that one text was the direct source for another, but it does recognize that texts from quite different communities and traditions participate in various ways in common cultural contexts and interact with various other texts.

We can make several observations about this network or cultural intertextuality.

First to be noted is that I, as the author of this book, am responsible for creating this intertextuality or network between Gospel texts and Roman imperial texts. I have selected these texts and placed them alongside each other thereby creating the opportunity for us to make meaning in the intersections among them. We have no way of knowing whether the authors of these texts ever intended them to be placed together. But as we know from social media, authors of spoken comments, emails, texts, and tweets do not control the reception of their messages. Cultural intertextuality is reader-centric, not author-centric.[2]

Second, I restrict my selection of texts to a particular time period and region, namely the first and early second centuries of the Common Era and the Roman Empire. I have not identified all the texts from the Roman Empire. Nor have I included texts from other contexts such as the tenth or fifteenth or eighteenth or twenty-first centuries. Doing so would be very interesting in creating different intertextualities or networks of relationships and interpretations. But doing so would open up an endless exercise in

---

1. Alkier, "Intertextuality and the Semiotics of Biblical Texts"; Allen, *Intertextuality*.

2. Moyise, "Intertextuality," 33–40.

meaning-making, which is far beyond the scope and focus of this book.

My focus is restricted for several reasons. One reason is pragmatic, the length and focus of this book. More importantly, in this book I am interested in thinking about the New Testament writings as participants in networks of texts from the Roman Empire in the first and second centuries CE. Often New Testament texts are considered only in relation to Jewish traditions. Here, I am interested in the cultural intertextuality between NT texts and texts created in the Roman Empire. How do the NT texts function in the company of other texts created by inhabitants of Rome's empire? What meanings do we make from these interactions?

Third, I employ an expansive understanding of the word "text." I use the word as it is commonly understood to refer to written documents. But also, I use "text" to refer to non-written "texts" such as monuments, buildings, statues, and coins that make statements about imperial power. Sometimes they incorporate words along with design and image, sometimes not.

Fourth, this choice of texts from the first and second centuries of the Roman Empire to constitute an intersecting network for interpreting NT texts leads to a foregrounding of imperial-political dimensions. This focus has not often been to the fore in interpreting the NT Gospels. Rather, Gospels have often been read as spiritualized, religious texts with no or little attention given to any cultural-political contexts or societal structures and practices. Or, scholars have often read the Gospels only in relation to Jewish cultural practices and understandings, thereby also underlining religious dimensions and artificiality refusing to recognize the imperial-political worlds that both Jewish texts and the

Gospel Texts Are Not Islands

Gospels negotiated.³ The four canonical Gospels emerged from powerful centers of imperial rule: Matthew's Gospel likely from Antioch, capital of the province of Syria; Mark's Gospel from Rome, the empire's capital; and John's Gospel perhaps from Ephesus, the capital of the province of Asia.⁴ Such cities are spaces that assert imperial-cultural values, visions, structures, and practices and that are peopled by imperial personnel. The Gospels' interactions with the cultural-political realities evident in these urban locations are inevitable and provide the focus for this book.

However, this study is not just an exercise in ancient history. My interest in these cultural-political intertextualities reflects my own location in and experiences with contemporary empires, as well as my concern to help us to think about the societal visions, practices, structures, and personnel of our own worlds. I spent the first half of my life in Aotearoa/New Zealand, a colony of the British empire. I lived at a time when the country was decolonizing itself and creating its own identity, impacted by its imperialized heritage yet charting an independent way in the world.

I have spent the second half of my life living in the most powerful empire that the world has ever seen, the USA. This nation combines enormous economic, military, and political-diplomatic reach and global presence with a profound confidence in its manifest destiny, that God has chosen and blessed the USA with the task of being the leader of the free world. This identity is, of course, ironic since the nation has enormous internal problems and challenges, such as pervasive racism, which the Black Lives Matter movement has highlighted, vast societal inequalities, extensive poverty, significant food insecurity, disparate

3. Moyise, "Intertextuality."

4. The place of origin of Luke's Gospel is much debated and unknown.

access to healthcare and quality education, questionable access to justice, subcultures of violence and anarchy ("white supremacy"), denigration of other nations, and so forth. These challenges, though, do not often seem to dent the self-constructed national identity of being the world's leader, even if other nations do not necessarily and readily accept such leadership.

I suggest that engaging the Gospels' intertextuality with the imperial-cultural texts of the Roman Empire foregrounds matters of societal visions, practices, structures, and personnel, both ancient and contemporary. Such intertextualities provoke us to think about the impact of the use of power and privilege in our world: How, for whom, and by whom are decisions made? Who has access to resources and opportunities? Who benefits and is privileged and who is harmed and excluded? What sort of societal visions, structures, and practices are in play?

THE ROMAN EMPIRE

Rome ruled an empire in the first-century CE of some sixty to sixty-five million people. Its territory extended around the Mediterranean Sea, along North Africa and Egypt, through Judea and Syria to the east, from (present-day) Turkey west across Europe including Greece, Italy, Germany, France, and Spain, and Britain in the north-west. Rome claimed control over people, land, sea, and production. We can note a number of features of this Roman imperial world.

Social hierarchy

The empire was *hierarchical* with vast disparities of power and wealth. A small elite group, some 2 to 3 percent of the population based in Rome and in provincial centers, accumulated and displayed great wealth in conspicuous consumption, exercised supreme political power, and exhibited elevated social status and privilege. They lived very comfortable and grandiose lives with their wealth, power, and status demonstrated, for example, in housing, clothing, economic activities, political offices, networks of elite allies, and numbers of slaves. Among these ruling elites, there were degrees of wealth. In the first century CE, the senatorial level required a property qualification of a million sesterces, equestrians required a property qualification of 400,000 sesterces, and decurions, who controlled local administration in cities and town, also had lower property qualifications. Emperors who were not willing to participate in partnerships with Roman and provincial elites usually met with unpleasant ends. These elite layers of the population contrasted with significant levels of poverty for many in the population.

Land-based wealth

The empire was *agrarian* in that elite wealth, power, and status were based predominantly in land and its productivity. Land holdings were frequently hereditary, sometimes contiguous, sometimes in dispersed locations. Absentee landowners were common so land was often worked by slaves under the oversight of a supervising slave (a *vilicus*) or leased to tenant farmers. Elites secured production by means of taxes, tributes, and rents often paid in goods more than coin. To not pay taxes or tribute was considered to be rebellion and a refusal to recognize Roman sovereignty over land, sea, labor, and production. Elites supplemented their wealth and ensured cash flow by involvement with trade as well as receiving rents from living spaces and warehouses.

Networks of power

The empire maintained control through various means, including *alliances* and *patron-client relationships* with leading provincials. King Herod—famed for killing the babies of Bethlehem in Matt 2:16—ruled as a client king with Rome's sanction and furthered Roman interests in the eastern empire. Rome dispatched governors like Pontius Pilate to rule provinces. They did so in alliances with elite personnel in provincial cities like Antioch, Ephesus, Corinth, and Jerusalem. Local elites filled civic administrative positions as magistrates and council members.

Rhetoric

One of the skills elite men needed was training in *rhetoric*. The performance of speeches was crucial for persuading others to accept a particular perspective and/or support a course of action. Rhetoric was thus a means of accomplishing domination over others in competitive political matters.

Public good works

Provincial elites often performed and financed public works called *euergetism* ("good works"). These public works involved funding local buildings and public facilities, entertainments, food handouts, temples, imperial cult observances, and the honoring of local gods and goddesses. In these activities, elites competed with each other for public honor and favor as clients of the chief patron of the empire, the emperor. In an agonistic or competitive society, rewards for power were great and relationships between provincials and Rome complex, involving deference, self-assertion, displays of wealth and loyalty, interdependence, and tensions.

Patriarchal

The empire was *patriarchal*. Through the first century all emperors were males. Elite men comprised senatorial and equestrian ranks and occupied positions of power in imperial and civic administration. This is not to say that there were no powerful women. Mothers and wives of emperors performed significant power often behind the scenes. Among these women were Livia, the wife of Emperor Augustus and mother of the next emperor, Tiberius, Messalina the third wife of Emperor Claudius, and Agrippina the fourth wife of Emperor Claudius and mother of the Emperor Nero.

Powerful and wealthy women were also prominent figures in cities throughout the empire. Plancia Magna (Plancia the "Great One"), for example, was very prominent in Perge in southern Asia Minor. Independently wealthy, she funded a complex of a city gates involving two towers, a two-story curving wall with niches for twenty-eight statues, and a triple-arched entrance. The statues represented herself as well as deified Emperors Nerva and Trajan, the living Emperor Hadrian, and numerous imperial women. Plancia was the priestess of Artemis Pergaia, of the Great Mother goddess, and of the imperial cult. These positions required her to lead and fund civic ceremonies that honored these deities, secured their blessing, expressed loyalty to Rome, and elevated Plancia's status and power.[5]

Plancia was not unique. Other such women included Eumachia of the southern Italian town of Pompeii. She was associated with and honored in a large building of prime downtown real estate located in Pompeii's forum.[6]

---

5. Boatwright, "Plancia Magna."
6. Cooley, *Pompeii*, 140–45.

Military power

Military action was another way that Rome and especially its elite males exhibited and accomplished dominance. Experience in war as an officer was an important step toward civic and political office. Success in military campaigns signified manly courage and domination over enemies. These values of manly dominance, power, and success were particularly celebrated in the "triumph," the victory parade accorded a victorious general when he returned to Rome after a military campaign. The Emperor Vespasian and his son Titus, victorious generals in Judea in 70 CE, paraded captives (slaves) and booty taken in battle, executed the captured enemy leader, and gave thanks to the appropriate deities. Roman power was *legionary,* with its military might upholding Roman domination, conquering power, hierarchical societal order, and divine blessing.

Blessings of the gods

Rome's dominance was maintained by a claim of *divine sanction*. Rome claimed to have been chosen by the gods, notably Jupiter, and commissioned to create and rule "an empire without end" (Virgil, *Aeneid* 1.278-79). Coins often displayed an image of the emperor on one side and on the other a deity, such as the goddess of victory (*Nike/Victoria*), to show the power behind the throne and to construct the emperor as the agent of the gods. The gods had selected Rome to manifest the gods' rule, presence, and favor. Submission to Rome, either voluntarily or forced through military conquest, was understood to comply with the divine will. Observances of the imperial cult in local communities and trade associations, whether in prayers and offerings to statues and temples, incense, vows, processions, festivals, meals, and games sought to please the gods and ensure continued blessing on the empire. The Emperor Augustus claims to have restored eighty-two temples in Rome as a display of piety intended to garner the ongoing favor and blessing of the gods (*Res Gestae* 20). Throughout the empire, elites played a prominent part in such activities, as leaders and priests or priestesses, and funders of buildings/temples and celebrations.

Slavery

The empire's elite controlled and benefitted from a *slave economy*. It is not clear how many slaves populated the empire. Estimates suggest somewhere between 20 and 30 percent of the population of perhaps sixty to sixty-five million. Slaves came from two sources, those born into slavery and those taken captives in military defeats. Slave labor and conditions were very varied. Many slaves worked on the land or in mines or in transportation (boats, wagons), others in households as cooks, cleaners, and groomers, yet others with skills and education worked in estate management, business and trade, medicine and teaching. Some masters and mistresses were harsh with severe (corporal) punishments, demanding working conditions, and minimal food and living conditions. Other owners were more humane in treating slaves as economic assets.

Jerry Toner identifies a range of stressors to which slaves were commonly subjected.[7] For many, sexual availability to masters and mistresses was a constant. Physical beatings, whether with fists, leather straps, whips, and/or rods, inflicted both pain and humiliation. Some slaves suffered from overwork while others endured boring roles and tasks. Some slaves were branded with TMQF (*tene me quia fuga*; "hold me because I am a runaway"). Foreign-born

7. Toner, *Popular Culture*, 54–74.

slaves suffered disorientation, loneliness, and isolation from homelands, loved ones, and a previous way of life. Children produced in slave partnerships were often removed from their parents by sale. If slaves were regarded as no longer useful, old and sick slaves could be freed and/or sold without any options and safeguards. Years of intimidation and brutalization left some slaves demoralized, deferential, and unassertive. Suicide provided one exit strategy for some slaves. For other slaves, there was the hope of being set free in manumission. Some freed men and women became successful and wealthy by means of business enterprises.

Non-elites

Much of the above discussion has been "top-down" in identifying elite means of political, economic, military, and ideological control. Yet the elites comprised only 2 or 3 percent of the population. Most inhabitants were non-elites living in varying degrees of poverty. Steven Friesen posited seven societal levels or degrees of wealth across the empire. Three levels concern elites, a fourth level comprises a comfortable middling group, and three levels demarcate degrees of poverty. Bruce Longenecker retained the seven levels but revised the percentages and renamed it as an economic scale.[8]

---

8. Friesen, "Poverty in Pauline Studies." Longenecker, *Remember the Poor*, 36–59.

Gospel Texts Are Not Islands

Scale	Category	Description	Percent: Friesen	Revised ES: Longenecker
PS1	Imperial Elites	Imperial dynasty, Roman senatorial families, a few retainers, local royalty, a few freed persons	0.04	ES 0.04
PS2	Regional or Provincial elites	Equestrian families, provincial officials, some retainers, some decurial families, some freed persons, some retired military officers	1.00	ES 1.00
PS3	Municipal Elites	Most decurial families, wealthy men and women who do not hold office, some freed persons, some retainers, some veterans, some merchants	1.76	ES 1.76
PS4	Those with moderate surplus	Some merchants and traders, freed persons, bankers, artisans who employ others, military veterans	7 (?)	ES 15

PS5	Stable Near Subsistence (with reasonable hope of remaining above the minimal level to sustain life)	Many merchants and traders, regular wage earners, artisans, large shop owners, freed persons, some farm families	22 (?)	ES 27
PS6	At subsistence level (often below minimum level to sustain life)	Small farm families, laborers (skilled and unskilled), artisans (those employed by others), wage earners, most merchants and traders, small shop and tavern owners	40	ES 30
PS7	Below subsistence Level	Some farm families, unattached widows, orphans, beggars, disabled, unskilled day laborers, prisoners	28	ES 25

While the two scholars vary somewhat in percentages for some categories (especially levels 4 and 6), both schemes resist a simplistic binary of rich and poor, of elite and non-elite. They identify seven levels of societal resources available to different groups. Some 80 percent (Longenecker) or 90 percent (Friesen) of the population knew significant degrees of poverty, with 55 to 70 percent (levels 6 and 7) frequently experiencing life below subsistence level. Their vulnerability was impacted by factors such as availability of work, yields from harvest, disease, weather, high prices, low wages, and civic stability. The majority of Jesus-followers belonged to levels 5 and 6, with perhaps a few from levels 4 and 7.

Urban living

Scholars have highlighted the unsanitary and difficult conditions in which many urban residents lived.[9] Intense population density is commonly linked with social conflicts and inter-personal violence. Poorly constructed tenement buildings often did not provide adequate light, ventilation, water supply, and sewage disposal. Cesspits existed in kitchens; latrines, where they existed, lacked washing facilities, and everywhere there was a fatal and fundamental ignorance of basic hygiene. Chamber pots were emptied in streets that were marked by disease-carrying insects and animals. Visits to public baths were often prescribed as medical treatments for fevers, paralysis, headaches, dysentery, worm infestations, bowel and anus troubles, gonorrhea, rabies, boils, and open sores, among others. Commenting on housing in Rome, Peter Brunt observes, "we may fairly suppose that most of the inhabitants . . . lived in appalling slums."[10]

Food insecurity and disease

Adding to the challenges of urban living was widespread food insecurity. Food reflected channels of power, with elites generally eating food of good quality, quantity, and

---

9. For the following, Aldrete, *Daily Life*, 75–106; Fagan, "Violence in Roman Social Relations," 467–95; Scobie, "Slums, Sanitation."

10. Brunt, "The Roman Mob," 13.

variety, while those in the lower societal levels had limited access to a variety of nutritionally adequate food.[11] Peter Garnsey argues that "for most people, life was a perpetual struggle for survival."[12]

One consequence of urban overcrowding, poor living conditions, and inadequate nutrition was high levels of disease. Particularly prevalent were diseases of deprivation and contagion.[13] The lack of adequate nutrition meant not only a lack of strength for physical work but also a lack of immunity against diseases and consequently high death rates. While establishing figures with any certainty is difficult because of the lack of sources, Bruce Frier points to the table of the third-century CE Roman jurist Ulpian, to census returns from Egypt, and to gravestone studies that suggest the average life expectancy at birth was about twenty-one or twenty-two years, and at age ten about thirty-five further years.[14] Ann Hanson suggests that "about half the babies born died before reaching their fifth birthday." Of those who reached age ten, nearly half reached age fifty. In overall terms, "less than twenty percent" reached sixty.[15]

Elite disdain

In addition to these challenges for much of the population of poor living conditions and of securing adequate resources, there is plenty of evidence for elites disdaining those below them in the societal hierarchy. One scholar compiles a four-page "lexicon of snobbery," a list of dignity-depriving

11. Aldrete and Mattingly, "Feeding the City"; Wilson, *For I Was Hungry*, 154–62.
12. Garnsey, *Food and Society*, xi.
13. Garnsey, *Food and Society*, 45.
14. Frier, "Roman Demography," 87–88.
15. Hanson, "The Roman Family," 27.

terms of abuse and insults with which elite writers referred to those of lower status.[16] Ironically, elites relied on the skills and labor of artisans and laborers from levels 4 to 6 (along with slaves) to uphold and enhance their wealth and status, even as they showed them little respect. Generally elites disdained manual labor. Its absence was one of numerous markers of elite identity. In addition, various tensions ran through society: between the powerful and the (relatively) powerless, the rich and (degrees of) the poor, inhabitants of Rome and provincials, male and female, urban and rural, and among ethnic groups.

Societal change?

Given these societal conditions of vast inequalities, did folks in levels 5 through 7 and slaves have any chance of changing the system? Were there widespread protests and violent attacks on elite personnel and property? Certainly there were outbursts of violent protests, ranging from slaves attacking and killing cruel masters; crowds protesting food shortages and demanding adequate supplies; crowds attacking an elite official; brigands or terrorists and pirates attacking elites and their property; and groups within nations who took up arms to revolt against Roman rule (e.g., Judea in 66–70 CE).[17]

But it would be erroneous to conclude that the absence of widespread violence and revolt meant everyone was happy to live under Roman rule. Social-scientist James Scott argues that responses of violent revolt and ready compliance do not exhaust the options for how people negotiate power. Scott explores how relatively powerless people make their way with various multivalent strategies, some

16. MacMullen, *Roman Social Relations*, 138–41.
17. Fagan, "Violence"; MacMullen, *Roman Social Relations*.

compliant, some resistant, some public, and some disguised and hidden.[18]

For example, practices of *material domination*, such as appropriating grain through taxes or coopting labor, might be met with public resistance such as boycotts, or with more disguised, self-protective, low-profile actions, such as poaching, squatting, foot-dragging, or hiding production. Practices of *status domination* that inflict humiliation, deny dignity, impose inferiority, and express insults toward the relatively powerless can be met with public counter-actions that assert dignity and desecrate status symbols associated with the ruling powerful. Or such practices can be met with private, disguised practices among the relatively powerless, such as tales of revenge, gossip, rituals, and assertions of dignity that develop in autonomous social spaces. Practices of *ideological domination* that claim (divine) justification for elite privilege, oppressive structures such as slavery, and structural injustice and poverty can be met with public counter-assertions that negate ruling ideologies and advocate more equitable perspectives and practices. Off-stage, dissident sub-cultures develop alternative narratives and perspectives that envision millennial or eschatological world-upside-down scenarios to counter (and reinscribe aspects of) the dominant ideology.

CONCLUSION

The New Testament writings participate in this system of imperial domination, even though they are not public writings. They are addressed to communities of Jesus-followers. In places they appear to submit to and cooperate with imperial rule. But they also dissent from Rome's societal vision, practices, and structures by imagining and advocating

18. Scott, *Domination*, 198 for a summary diagram.

alternative commitments and ways of being human shaped by God's purposes and Jesus' teaching. Yet even in offering alternative visions, the Gospels can imitate and reinscribe imperial language, structures, and practices. The NT writings negotiate imperial systems in multiple ways.

Moreover, I argue that the Gospels imitate various imperial strategies that present elite ruling men as divinely sanctioned rulers in showing Jesus as a divinely sanctioned agent not of the empire of Rome but of the empire of God. Yet while the imperial accounts construct imperial men to embody and uphold imperial practices and structures, the Gospel accounts construct Jesus sometimes participating in, sometimes imitating, sometimes dissenting from, and sometimes providing alternatives to the structures and behaviors of Rome's elite males.

DISCUSSION QUESTIONS

1. What is intertextuality and how does this approach contribute to understanding the Gospels?
2. If you were a member of the Roman Empire's elite (male or female), how would you describe the structures, practices, and vision of the empire from which you benefit?
3. If you were a member of the Roman Empire's non-elite (for example, level 6; a slave), how would you describe your experiences of living in the Roman Empire?

2

GOSPELS AND ANCIENT BIOGRAPHIES

WHAT SORT OF TEXTS are we reading when we read the New Testament Gospels? Some readers have thought of the Gospels as eyewitness accounts, or "a day in the life of Jesus" narratives, or "Dear Diary" moments. None of these approaches is accurate. None of the Gospels claims to be eyewitness accounts, the names associated with two of the Gospels (Mark, Luke) are not identified among the twelve male followers of Jesus, and several of the followers associated with Jesus' inner circle are not claimed to be Gospel authors (Peter, James, Andrew). And the Gospels disagree on central aspects of their presentations of Jesus' activity: they do not agree on the names of Jesus twelve male followers (compare Matt 10:1-4; Luke 6:12-16), only Matthew's Gospel has Jesus preach the Sermon on the Mount (Matt 5-7), only John's Gospel has Jesus offering lengthy teaching before his passion (John 13-17) and journeying back and forth between Galilee and Jerusalem while the other

Gospels and Ancient Biographies

Gospels concentrate Jesus' activity in Galilee before a final journey to Jerusalem (Mark 10; Matt 19–20; Luke 9–19).

Yet along with these differences, the New Testaments Gospels have significant features in common with each other

- In each Gospel Jesus is the main character and the focus of the accounts. He is the subject of around 20 percent of the verbs, and commonly the object of actions. Other characters (Jerusalem leaders; followers; crowds) are positioned in relation to him.

- All the Gospels narrate Jesus' activity in a general chronological sequence that also incorporates thematic collections of material. Matthew and Luke begin with Jesus' conception and birth. All include the witness of John the Baptist and Jesus' baptism (including John 1:31–34?). All focus on Jesus' calling disciples, teaching, and miracles. Actions happen in Galilee and Jerusalem in the context of the Roman Empire. Thematic collections include teachings of a particular genre and subject (parables, Mark 4; Luke 15:1—16:13; eschatological material, Matt 24–25). All end with Jesus' death by crucifixion at the hands of an alliance of Jerusalem leaders and the Roman governor Pilate. Events leading up to and involving Jesus' death and resurrection concern some 15 to 20 percent of the Gospel narratives.

- Jesus' actions, interactions with other characters, and his teachings reveal his character. His virtues include compassion with crowds, his willingness to confront the powerful Jerusalem-based, Rome-sanctioned leaders over their societal structures and practices, and loyal and steadfast devotion to God's will. The Gospels commonly narrate his actions in short episodes. His teachings emerge in both short exchanges and protracted monologues. Combined, they offer a vision of human existence and practices in accord with divine purposes.

- The Gospels employ prose narratives, not poems or philosophical discourses.
- The Gospels generally adopt a serious tone and construct the narrative of Jesus' life with considerable respect.
- The Gospels teach readers about Jesus and shape the identity, commitments, practices, and lifestyle of his followers. They expose opponents of his teaching and actions, criticize the societal visions, practices, and personnel of the Roman world, and advocate for the different understandings and practices of faithful following.

GOSPELS AS ANCIENT BIOGRAPHIES

These features in a literary work—concentrated focus on a main character, chronological sequence, actions and interactions that disclose character, the use of prose, a serious and respectful tone, the shaping of the identity, commitments, and lifestyle of followers—were not unique in the ancient world. In fact, they were features of a genre called "ancient biography," a type of writing that celebrated the values and accomplishments of elite males in the Roman world. These ancient biographies often averaged fifteen to twenty thousand words in length as do the Gospels.

What takes place in the intertextuality between the Gospels and ancient biographies?

These ancient biographies differed from modern "kiss-and-tell" biographies. The latter concern themselves with the internal growth of their subject, the development of a particular personality, entertainment through scandals and salacious incidents, shocking relationships, unusual experiences. Ancient biographies allowed for some development of character and personality, but attention centered much more on the external actions and words that expressed the main character's virtuous qualities and characteristics. Richard Burridge explains:

> The methods of ancient characterization were much more indirect than their modern counterparts. Detailed character analysis and psychological assessment are lacking, not just in the gospels, but in the bulk of ancient literature. Instead, character is revealed by the person's words and deeds, especially the latter: as Aristotle put it, "actions are signs of character" (*Rhetoric* I.ix.33. 1367b).[1]

These biographies set forth virtues for their audience to admire and emulate, sometimes by contrast in presenting vices and failings. The subjects of these biographies—usually eminent men who were philosophers, generals, and rulers—were not constructed as unique individuals of outstanding abilities. Rather they were constructed as representatives of elite male values and virtues. In displaying manly values of domination and courage, ancient biographies commended a positive view of the imperial world under Roman control.

---

1. Burridge, *What Are the Gospels?* 117, also 139; "there is a high degree of correlation between the generic features of Graeco-Roman *bioi* and those of the synoptic gospels. . . . [T]he synoptic gospels belong within the overall genre of *bioi*" (212).

Ancient biographies: Suetonius

One writer of ancient biographies was Gaius Suetonius (c 70 CE–c.130 CE). Suetonius, perhaps born in Hippo in North Africa, wrote a series of biographies of Roman literary men such as grammarians, rhetoricians, poets, and historians. More well-known is his set of twelve biographies of Roman emperors from Julius Caesar to Domitian.[2] Suetonius combines a chronological ordering of his material with topical organization. The biographies begin with ancestry and early life, pre-accession career (political offices, military campaigns) and accomplishments as emperor. Suetonius seems especially interested in public works (buildings; entertainments), administration of justice and governance, territorial acquisition through military campaigns, financial generosity to some subjects, personal qualities (mercy, self-control, piety, courage), idiosyncrasies, and failings (sexual; arrogance; cruelty; avarice) as he upheld his ideal of Roman power by warning of the dangers of hereditary rule and tyranny. Anecdotes filled out the presentation along with a description of physical appearance and self-presentation. Biographies ended with a sustained focus on the subject's death.[3]

Ancient biography: Tacitus

Another example is the biography that Tacitus wrote about his father-in-law, Agricola. The biography was written in 98 CE, five years after Agricola's death and close to the time when the Gospels were written.[4] Consistent with the genre

   2. Bradley, "Introduction," *Suetonius*, 12–27.
   3. Burridge, *What Are the Gospels?* 150–84.
   4. Burridge (*What Are the Gospels?* 151 note 6) notes disputes concerning the genre of *Agricola*. He demonstrates its use of the generic features of biography (150–81).

of biography, this work displays Agricola's character "in what he did, so that the commemoration of individuals was in effect a record of their deeds."[5] Agricola was a member of the senatorial ruling elite. His career embraced various military and political positions mostly in Rome-occupied Britain where he was governor for seven years. Tacitus' construction of Agricola as a faithful representative of the empire is very positive. He celebrates Agricola's elite origins and the accomplishments of his ancestors. And he outlines Agricola's political and military accomplishments. Agricola's character is manifested in the deeds of his political career, his aggressive and territorially expansive governorship in Britain and Scotland, his rhetoric and advocacy of Roman ways, his administrative skill, his military success, including his decisive victory in 84 CE over the British tribes under the leadership of Calgacus at Mount Graupius (*Agricola* 29–39), and, especially, his ability to negotiate with moderation the tyrannical and jealous rule of the Emperor Domitian. He accomplished the latter by his faithful and loyal attention to his political and military duties in subjugating Britons on behalf of Rome without being distracted or intimidated by Domitian's responses. Burridge observes that Agricola's "character is depicted through the description of events."[6] The deeds that Tacitus narrates exemplify elite manly qualities: Agricola's self-control, his dominance over land and peoples, his courage or *virtus* demonstrated in ruling and warfare, his duty and loyalty to the Roman Empire, his astute negotiation of difficult circumstances of Emperor Domitian's power.

Significantly, these qualities are not unique to Agricola. Tacitus' narrative presents Agricola as a manly man who exhibited characteristics that are typical of constructions

5. Hutton, *Tacitus*, 18.
6. Burridge, *What Are the Gospels?* 170.

of elite masculinity in the Roman world, a man of lineage, wealth, power, status, domination over others, and courage (*virtus*),[7] a man who advocated and was faithful to Rome's identity and mission as the rulers of the world. Narrated actions display his exemplary manly elite character.

Features of ancient biographies

Richard Burridge identifies four clusters of textual features typical of ancient biographies:

1. *Features of the biography's beginning:* Biographies usually begin with a title and an opening formula, or preface, or prologue.

2. *Distinctive focus:* The biography's focus falls on the main character. He is the main subject and/or object of the verbs. Other characters function in relation to him. The subject matter or content concerns him.

3. *Features of the biography's form:* Ancient biographies are prose narratives with an average length of ten to twenty thousand words. Their style is straightforward with a generally serious and respectful tone. Their subject matter usually concerns an elite male, such as a ruler, emperor, and military commander. The biography usually employs an overarching chronological structure moving from ancestry to death. Within this chronology, material might be arranged topically in providing examples of a particular behavior or accomplishment. Short episodes that display actions and teachings elaborate the subject's character. Biographies use and acknowledge sources for their information.

---

7. Williams, *Roman Homosexuality*, 145–70.

Gospels and Ancient Biographies

4. *Content of the biography:* The content focuses on the main character. Other characters and settings are used in relation to the construction of this character. Topics commonly include ancestry, birth, upbringing or training, great deed, virtues, death and its consequences. A tension between the real and the stereotypical can be in play. Attacks on enemies and opponents are usually designed to contrast with and foreground the virtues and accomplishments of the main character. Together, the content serves a purpose of informing, teaching, and persuading its audience.

These same four features are evident in the canonical Gospels.

1. *Features of the Gospel's beginnings:* Mark's Gospel begins with an opening formula: "The beginning of the good news of Jesus Christ, the Son of God" (Mark 1:1). Matthew's Gospel similarly begins with an opening formula: "An account of the genealogy of Jesus the Messiah, the son of David, the son of Abraham." Luke's Gospel begins a little differently with a narrative prologue that explains to Theophilus how the Gospel is written (after investigating previous accounts as sources) as well as why it is written: "so that you may know security (or certainty or assurance) concerning the things about which you have previously received instruction" (Luke 1:1–4, author's translation). John's Gospel also begins with a prologue but of a different kind. Instead of an explanation of the Gospel's purpose, John's much longer prologue provides a theological-pastoral reflection on the divine purposes that Jesus accomplishes (John 1:1–18).

2. *Distinctive focus:* The Gospels focus on and concentrate on Jesus as the main character. This focus is

evident in these opening statements. Mark introduces Jesus with two confessional terms, Christ ("anointed one") and son of God, a term that identifies Jesus as God's agent in intimate relationship with God (Mark 1:1). Matthew also identifies Jesus as the Messiah or Christ (Matt 1:1). Messiah and Christ are synonyms; Messiah derives from Hebrew while Christ derives from Greek. Both terms mean "anointed" or commissioned to serve God. Matthew also locates Jesus in relation to two key figures in Israel's traditions, Abraham through whom God promised to bless all the nations of the earth (Gen 12:3), and David whom God chose as king to represent divine purposes set out, for example, in Psalm 72. Luke begins by evoking God's actions and in that context introduces Jesus in verse 31 when the angel announces to Mary that she will conceive a son who is to be named Jesus. John's opening prologue names Jesus in verse 17, but he has been the subject throughout since verse 1. Throughout the Gospels, the focus remains on Jesus. In Mark, Jesus is subject of about 25 percent of the verbs. In Matthew and Luke, he is the subject of almost 20 percent of the verbs. In John, the percentage is greater, over 30 percent. And as with other ancient biographies, the Gospels give comparable attention to Jesus' death, some 15 to 20 percent of the work.

3. *Features of the Gospel's form:* The Gospels consist of prose narratives in straightforward style and with respectful tone and regard for the subject. Their length between eleven and twenty thousand words falls within the average for medium-length biographies. All four Gospels employ an overarching chronological structure though there are some significant differences in the chronologies. Mark begins with John the Baptist

Gospels and Ancient Biographies

(Mark 1:2-8). Matthew (Matt 1:1-17) and Luke (Luke 3:23-38) set out genealogies for Jesus, though they differ in the lines of ancestry they trace. Matthew (chs 1-2) and Luke (chs 1-2) narrate the conception and birth of Jesus. John locates Jesus' origin with God "in the beginning" (John 1:1-2). Luke's Gospel alone includes an incident involving Jesus' boyhood (Luke 2:41-52). Three of the Gospels (Matthew, Mark, Luke) locate Jesus' activity in Galilee until he goes to Jerusalem to die. John's Gospel has Jesus moving regularly between Galilee and Jerusalem.

Within this chronological framework, the Gospels use topical organization to emphasize aspects of Jesus' activity. Collections of short episodes comprising miracle stories (healings, exorcisms, feedings) feature in Mark 1:21—2:12 and Matt 8-9. A concentration of conflict stories in Matt 21-22 show Jesus getting the better of his opponents so that no one "dared to ask him any more questions" (Matt 22:46). Likewise, there are collections of his teachings such as Luke's sermon the plain (Luke 6:20-49), parables (Mark 4; Luke 15), eschatological scenarios (Mark 13; Matt 24-25), and instructions for being a follower in Jesus' absence (John 13-17). Through these accounts of Jesus' actions and teachings, the Gospels like ancient biographies manifest Jesus' character. Each Gospel ends with accounts of Jesus' death and its consequences in his resurrection. Mark's account is a brief eight verses with Matt 28, Luke 24, and John 20-21 considerably expanding the length of the resurrection accounts.

In constructing their narratives, the Gospels use sources. Scholars have demonstrated that both Matthew and Luke use Mark's Gospel as a source as well as a collection of Jesus' teaching called "Q," an abbreviation of the German word for source, *Quelle*.[8] The opening of Luke's Gospel acknowledges these sources:

> Since many have undertaken to set down an orderly account of the events that have been fulfilled among us, just as they were handed on to us by those who from the beginning were eyewitnesses and servants of the word, I too decided, after investigating everything carefully from the very first, to write an orderly account for you, most excellent Theophilus. (Luke 1:1–3)

4. *Content of the Gospels:* The central focus on Jesus as the main character has been indicated in section 3. His actions and teachings disclose his virtues and character. Jesus' interaction with his disciples, such as calling and teaching them, also highlights aspects of his character: his dominating authority, his access to and teaching of the divine will, his disclosure of the eschatological goals, his shaping of a community with its distinctive practices of mercy and love. He interacts with both male followers (Mark 3:13–19) and women followers (Mark 15:40–41; Luke 8:1–3). His conflicts with the Rome-sanctioned, Jerusalem-based alliance of leaders highlight different societal visions, structures, and practices that repair the damage of the imperial world (Luke 1:51–53; 4:18–19; 6:20–26) and contrast imperial practices in commending service instead of domination (Mark 10:41–44), not pursuing wealth and status (Matt 6:24; Luke 14:7–24), the practice of mercy (Luke 16:19–31; Matt 25:31–46), the inclusion of social outsiders (Matt 5:43–48; 9:10–13; Luke 15), the doing of justice, mercy, and faithfulness

---

8. Carter, *Matthew: Storyteller*, 30–65.

Gospels and Ancient Biographies

(Matt 23:23), and renouncing violence (Matt 26:51–53; 5:9).

Crowds typically provide receptive audiences for Jesus' teaching and gifts of healing and food (Mark 6:30–56), though a Jerusalem crowd under the sway of its leaders calls for Jesus' crucifixion (Luke 23:13–25). In his characteristic actions of conflict with opponents and teaching disciples and crowds, these typical virtues and practices coexist with real experiences such as Jesus' inability to control circumstances (Mark 1:45), his anger (Mark 3:5), ignorance (Mark 5:9; 6:38; 9:16), compassion (Matt 9:36), being tired and thirsty (John 4:6–7), and grieving (John 11:35). Settings in the narrative provide contexts for Jesus' actions, teachings, and conflicts (wilderness, mountain, houses, synagogues, lake, village, Jerusalem, temple). The content of the Gospels commends Jesus, elaborates his teaching, actions, and characteristics, instructs followers on how to follow him, inspires faithful following, counters misunderstandings, and discredits opponents.

Significant similarities exist between the features of ancient biographies and the canonical Gospels. Burridge comments, "the ancient method was to display character through deeds and words. This is precisely what we find in the evangelists' characterization of Jesus."[9]

A COUPLE OF GOSPEL SURPRISES

Yet in a couple of distinct and surprising, even subversive ways, the Gospels depart from important conventions and characterizations of ancient biographies.

---

9. Burridge, *What Are the Gospels?* 199.

Jesus: not an elite male

First, the Gospels do not imitate the focus of these ancient biographies on males of elevated social status and accomplishment. Biographies focused on powerful males such as rhetoricians, emperors, and successful ruling and conquering figures. These individuals exhibited elite masculine cultural values in support of imperial practices of dominating and ruling over others. Philo presents Moses as a king. Tacitus emphasizes Agrippa's accomplishments as a military and political leader. Suetonius features twelve emperors.

But the Gospels focus on Jesus. He is not an elite figure. His household is not a high status family of social standing, wealth, networks, influence, and accomplishments. The Gospels present his origin from small villages in Roman-subjugated Galilee, Bethlehem (Luke 2:4–6), Nazareth (Matt 2:23; Luke 4:16), and Capernaum (Matt 4:13). And they are clear in constructing Jesus' non-elite, village-based, family origins:

> On the sabbath he began to teach in the synagogue, and many who heard him were astounded. They said, "Where did this man get all this? What is this wisdom that has been given to him? What deeds of power are being done by his hands! Is not this the carpenter, the son of Mary and brother of James and Joses and Judas and Simon, and are not his sisters here with us?" And they took offense at him. (Mark 6:2–3)

> He came to his hometown and began to teach the people in their synagogue, so that they were astounded and said, "Where did this man get this wisdom and these deeds of power? Is not this the carpenter's son? Is not his mother called Mary? And are not his brothers James

> and Joseph and Simon and Judas? And are not all his sisters with us? Where then did this man get all this?" And they took offense at him. (Matt 13:54–57)

> All spoke well of him and were amazed at the gracious words that came from his mouth. They said, "Is not this Joseph's son?" (Luke 4:22)

> They were saying, "Is not this Jesus, the son of Joseph, whose father and mother we know? How can he now say, 'I have come down from heaven'?" (John 6:42)

> The Jews were astonished at it, saying, "How does this man have such learning, when he has never been taught?" (John 7:15)

From these citations, several observations about how the Gospels construct Jesus' origins and status emerge:

- He is identified as the carpenter's son (Mark 6:3; Matt 13:55). Both his mother Mary (Mark 6:3) and his father Joseph (Luke 4:22; John 6:42) are specifically named. Given his father's occupation, Jesus probably trained as an apprentice carpenter.[10]

- He is well known among the locals in these small villages. He is not an outsider who has come to these villages. He was raised in these locations

- His family, namely his brothers and sisters, are well known to other villagers by name.

- The locals are surprised by his learning when he has not received rhetorical training or education (John 7:15; Luke 4:22).

---

10. Huebner, *Papyri*, 81–82.

Sabine Huebner uses the documentary papyri of Greco-Roman Egypt to elaborate the Greek term translated "carpenter" (*tektōn*).[11] The documents associate the word "carpenter" with building "roof structures for houses . . . oil mills, furniture, wagons, chariots, wheels, . . . barges and boats, . . . mechanized wooden water wheels, . . . wooden doors and window, . . . towers, storage facilities military defense walls, bridges and siege machines."[12] In payment lists, carpenters appear with "lower craftsmen and day laborers, freedmen, and slaves," perhaps earning around fifty sesterces a month.[13] Accordingly, readers of the Gospels would understand Jesus as originating in a lower-status craftsman household that was probably somewhat better off than unskilled workers. Huebner estimates that a household such as that to which Joseph and Jesus belonged had at least some minimal ability in the literacy necessary to sustain their business.

Clearly the Gospels do not construct Jesus as a high-status male elite from a leading family. He is from small villages in a province under Roman rule. As is true of persons experiencing degrees of subjugation to imperial rule, the Gospels show him negotiating Roman power with a mixture of simultaneous strategies spanning accommodation, resistance in imagining alternative worlds, coopting imperial paradigms, and repairing imperial damage.

Yet even in this imperial context, the Gospels also construct him as a person of some societal influence that extends far beyond a village craft worker's household in the Galilee. He attracts followers or disciples who want to learn from him. The Greek term translated as "disciple" literally denotes a learner or student. He draws crowds from not

11. Huebner, *Papyri*, 65–86.
12. Huebner, *Papyri*, 66.
13. Huebner, *Papyri*, 67, 79.

Gospels and Ancient Biographies

only the Galilee but also from Syria (Matt 4:24). At the end of Matthew's Gospel, the Matthean Jesus employs a very imperial practice in requiring his followers to "make disciples of all nations" and spread his teaching everywhere (Matt 28:20).[14] In front of disciples and benefitting crowds, Jesus displays his restorative and dominating power over disease in healings, demons in exorcisms, and food scarcity with feedings. He exercises dominating power over nature in calming storms. In his teachings, his rhetoric exercises domination over people's minds, worldviews, and ways of life as he provokes hearers to imagine a different way of life and identity in the purposes of God. His powerful rhetoric also announces curses or words of judgment on the rich and satisfied (Luke 6:24–26), on the Rome-sanctioned scribes and Pharisees (Matt 23:13–36), on Jerusalem and the Roman Empire (Mark 13; Matt 24), and on all nations that do not care for the societally vulnerable and damaged (Matt 25:31–46).

The Gospels construct Jesus' power and authority as divinely sanctioned. Mark's Gospel introduces Jesus in the company of five male characters who were divine representatives: Isaiah, Moses, Malachi, Elijah, John the Baptist. Then God declares Jesus to be God's son or agent (Mark 1:1–11).[15] Matthew's Gospel opens with the angel of the Lord declaring Jesus' mission to manifest God's saving presence (Matt 1:21–23). Luke's Gospel opens with a similar commissioning scene at Jesus' conception:

> . . . and you will name him Jesus. He will be great, and will be called the Son of the Most High, and the Lord God will give to him the throne of his

---

14. Compare the longer ending of Mark 16:15, where the same command occurs. The longer ending comprising Mark 16:8–20 was added probably in the later second or early third century.

15. Carter, *Mark*, 1–10.

ancestor David. He will reign over the house of
Jacob forever, and of his kingdom there will be
no end. (Luke 1:31–33)

John's Gospel locates Jesus "in the beginning" with God who sends him to earth. Jesus' power and authority are recognized in the language that the Gospels use for him. Terms of address such as "Lord" signify his domination while "son of God" signifies his role as God's agent. Jesus has both insignificant origins as well as dominating power.

Jesus' death by crucifixion

Second, the Gospels imitate the attention on Jesus' death that is a feature of ancient biographies. Biographies generally played out a cultural script of the "good" or "noble death." This death meant the courageous acceptance of its circumstances and inevitable outcome. It was accompanied by honor for the biography's subject. Dying bravely was the expectation. I will elaborate this notion of a noble death in chapter 8.

Here the Gospels go off script somewhat. At first glance, Jesus' death is *not* noble; it is death by crucifixion. Crucifixion was a death penalty for criminals. Moreover, it enacted a political and imperial death penalty. It was not a death penalty used for Roman citizens (Cicero, *Pro Rabirio* 9–17, except for treason). Rather it was used for outsiders and nobodies like "rebellious" foreigners (Josephus, *J.W.* 2.306–8; 5.449–53; Philo, *In Flaccum* 72, 84), violent criminals and robbers (Martial, *On the Spectacles* 9), and slaves (Cicero, *In Verrine* 2.5.162; Juvenal, *Sat* 6.219–24; Tacitus, *Ann* 13.32.1). Jesus' death by crucifixion associates him with such social outsiders. It was regarded as a cruel and demeaning form of execution (Tacitus, *Ann* 15.44.4; Seneca, *De Ira* 1.2.2). Josephus calls it the "most pitiable of deaths" (*J.W.* 7.203). It signified shame, humiliation, pain, socio-political rejection, condemnation, death, and the unmanning of masculinity at the hands of more powerful men. Crucifixions were carried out in popular public places with the crucified victim, male and female, naked and shamed. Crucifixions had intimidating force, a visual display to subjugated provincials of the futility of challenge to Roman rule.

Most of the time the Gospels present Jesus approaching his death steadfastly, choosing to go to Jerusalem where he conflicts with the ruling alliance of Jerusalem leaders and Pilate. Yet in Gethsemane, his resolve wavers as he asks God to spare him from this death (Mark 14:36). His followers run away and abandon him. He dies alone, deserted, mocked as a kingly wannabe, subjugated to Roman power.

Yet the Gospels re-present and reframe this expression of imperial violence and intimidation. It becomes a symbol of faithfulness to God's purposes (Mark 8:34). And it comes to be a site that reveals the limits and weakness of Roman power. Rome cannot keep Jesus dead. God's power prevails in raising Jesus from the dead. This reframing of crucifixion is an instance of the technique of catachresis whereby colonized peoples deconstruct imperial dominance and recast its instruments in terms of contest and subversion.[16]

CONCLUSION

The Gospels employ features of a genre that we know as ancient biographies. With ancient biographies, Gospels concentrate focus on a main character, employ a chronological sequence, disclose the character of the main figure in his actions and interactions, use prose and a serious and

16. Leander, *Discourses of Empire*, 245–49, employing the concept from Gayatri Spivak.

respectful tone, set forth these virtues for audiences to admire and emulate and to shape the identity, commitments, and lifestyle of followers. In displaying representative elite manly values and practices of domination and courage, ancient biographies commended a positive view of the imperial world under Roman control. The Gospels locate Jesus in this cultural mix, but dissent from it in several significant ways: They emphasize Jesus' lowly origins as a provincial under Roman rule who lacks societal status. They portray his death by the highly dishonorable event of crucifixion.

Subsequent chapters will examine further aspects of the Gospels' construction of Jesus in relation to this and other cultural codes.

DISCUSSION QUESTIONS

1. Why does identifying the genre of a literary work or film or TV series matter? Have you had the experience of misidentifying or confusing genres in choosing a book or TV series?

2. What are the features of an ancient biography? What features does Tacitus' biography of his father-in-law Agricola exhibit? And what features do the Gospels share with ancient biographies?

3. The chapter notes some "surprises" in how the Gospels depart from the standard features of ancient biographies. What are they?

4. What effect does it have to read the Gospels as ancient biographies and not, for example, as eye-witness accounts? What can we expect and not expect from reading the Gospels in this way?

3

ORIGINS

We humans construct our identities in numerous ways. We might do it by naming our familial roles: mother, son, grandparent, daughter, father. We might do it by naming relationships: friend, partner, employee. We might do it by naming our occupation: I am a nurse, a teacher, a farmer, an administrative assistant, an IT person, a housebuilder. We might do it by naming our place of origin, whether a country, state, city, town, or neighborhood. We might do it by naming our ethnicity or gender. We might do it by naming famous or notorious ancestors: my great-grandfather started this very successful business; this relative was a famous sportsperson or artist or economist or politician; this relative was a felon.

CONSTRUCTING IDENTITY FROM ORIGINS

The Roman world also utilized some of these ways of constructing identity. Especially common was to signal greatness by attending to an elite man's origins, whether by claiming divine action, genealogy, adoption, and identifying ancestors distinguished by various accomplishments.[1] Not surprisingly, the Gospels employ similar strategies of genealogy, divine action, adoption, and ancestry in constructing Jesus' identity. What arises in the intersectionality between Roman constructions of male greatness and the Gospel's construction of Jesus' identity?

In this chapter, we begin with identifying some of the ways in which the origins of eminent Roman figures were utilized to underscore their greatness. Then we'll look at ways in which the Gospels intersect with these strategies, reinscribing or imitating them, as well as diverging from them, in constructing Jesus' identity by various combinations of genealogy, divine action, adoption, and human ancestors.

The origins of Emperor Augustus

The importance of an impressive genealogy for defining the identity and status of a dominant man is reflected in Suetonius' biography of the Emperor Augustus. Suetonius supplies three accounts of Augustus' origins to bolster the latter's greatness. Suetonius makes no attempt to reconcile the different accounts.

One construction of Augustus' origin involves adoption. The militarily successful and politically powerful figure Julius Caesar adopted Augustus as his heir and successor in his will read after his murder in 44 BCE. Caesar's adopting of Octavian-Augustus as his heir and successor opened the way for Augustus' subsequent attainment of supreme power as emperor after eliminating his rival Mark Antony in the battle of Actium in 31 BCE.

1. Wiseman, "Legendary Genealogies"; Thomas, "Genealogy"; Kurz, "Luke 3:23–38"; Talbert, "Miraculous Conceptions."

Origins

Caesar's genealogy traced back to Aeneas and his son Iulus/Ascanius; Aeneas was the son of Venus.[2] Caesar's adoption of Augustus not only associates him with Julius Caesar but also places him in this line of power and privilege that originates with the goddess Venus and one of Rome's founding ancestors, Aeneas.[3]

> Then at the request of his father-in-law, Lucius Piso, the will was unsealed and read in Antony's house.... At the end of the will, too, he adopted Gaius Octavius into his family and gave him his name. (Suetonius, *Deified Julius* 82–83; *Deified Augustus* 7; 94.11).[4]

Subsequently the Senate upgraded Caesar's identity and status in declaring him divine:

> Instead of a eulogy the consul Antonius caused a herald to recite the decree of the Senate in which it had voted Caesar all divine and human honours at once.... He died in the fifty-sixth year of his age, and was numbered among the gods, not only by a formal decree, but also in the conviction of the common people. For at the first of the games which his heir Augustus gave in honour of his apotheosis, a comet shone for seven successive days . . . and was believed to be the soul of Caesar, who had been taken to heaven. (Suetonius, *Deified Julius* 88)

---

2. Suetonius, *Julius* 6.1; Dio, *Roman History*, 41.34.1.

3. Peppard, *Son of God*, 46–49, also 50–85.

4. Other emperors are adopted into illustrious family lines. Augustus adopts Tiberius as his successor (Suetonius, *Tiberius* 15, 21, 23); Tiberius adopts his nephew Gaius Caligula as his successor (Suetonius, *Tiberius* 76; *Gaius Caligula* 1); Claudius adopts Nero (Suetonius, *Nero* 6, 7); Galba adopts Piso Frugi Licinianus (Suetonius, *Galba* 17).

Augustus' adoption by Julius Caesar and the subsequent divinization of Caesar allowed Augustus to be known as "son of a god." Virgil places Augustus among the descendants of Aeneas and identifies "Caesar Augustus, son of a god" (*Aeneid* 6.788–94). Inscriptions in both Latin (*divi filius*) and Greek in the East (*theou huios*) attest this identity and status.[5] This title secured the perception of an alliance between Augustus and the gods, thereby constructing Augustus as the agent or representative of the gods and their will. It identified, sanctioned, and empowered his assertions of imperial power and godlike authority as emperor. It impressed and cowered his subjects, securing appropriate honor and obedience. Who wants to risk resisting one whom the gods have chosen?

Crucial to note, then, is that adoption is not inferior to biological descent. It is equally a path to prestige, power, domination, and greatness.[6]

Suetonius provides a second account of Augustus' origin, namely his divine begetting.[7] Ovid declares that Augustus was not "born of mortal seed."[8] Suetonius narrates how Augustus is conceived when the god Apollo impregnates Augustus' mother, Atia, the niece of Julius Caesar.

> When Atia had come in the middle of the night
> to the solemn service of Apollo, she had her litter set down in the temple and fell asleep, while

---

5. For example, inscriptions from Ephesus identify Augustus as "son of a god" (*I.Eph* 2.252, 253; 5.1522, 1523, 1524).

6. Peppard, *Son of God*, 93–95.

7. For discussion of the fate of claims of "descent from gods" through the first century, Hesketh, "Descendants of Gods." Some writers (Plutarch, *Numa Pompilius* 21.4; Seneca, *De Beneficiis* 3.28.2) place little credence in claims of ancestries from gods, with Seneca claiming people "slip in a god" into their ancestry in the absence of distinguished ancestors.

8. Ovid, *Metamorphoses* 15.760.

Origins

the rest of the matrons also slept. Suddenly a serpent glided up to her and shortly went away.[9] When she awoke, she purified herself, as if after the embraces of her husband, and at once there appeared on her body a mark in colours like a serpent, and she could never get rid of it; so that presently she ceased ever to go to the public baths. In the tenth month after that Augustus was born and was therefore regarded as the son of Apollo. (Suetonius, *Deified Augustus* 94.4; also Dio Cassius, *Roman History,* 45.2–3)

Begotten by Apollo, Augustus could claim divine origin not only as the son of the divine Julius but also as the son of Apollo. As a chief god, Apollo was understood to have many roles. Particularly relevant for Augustus was Apollo's protection in his battle with Mark Antony at Actium in 31 BCE for supreme power in the empire. Augustus enlarged a temple of Apollo near Actium to honor that power and blessing.[10] Apollo was also associated with founding new towns, dominion over inhabitants, and giving of laws and constitutions, all of which had great import for Augustus' actions in expanding Roman dominance.

But fundamentally, to be son of the god Apollo provided divine legitimation for Augustus and his ruling authority. It constructed him as a chosen agent of the supreme god, a recipient of his favor and power, a representative of the divine will. Such an emperor was to be honored and obeyed.

In addition to adoption and divine begetting, Suetonius provides a third account of Augustus' origins, namely his

---

9. A serpent often represented a person or people's *genius*, a deified concept of the power of generation, particularly the entirety of traits united in an individual, akin to the notion of the self. Scheid, "genius."

10. Suetonius, *Deified Augustus* 18.2.

biological descent from a distinguished family. The opening four sections of Suetonius' biography narrate the accomplishments of the Octavian family. The account starts with an ancient ancestor, devoted to Mars, who distinguished himself in military action. Further distinction is signaled by the family's admission to the Senate by the legendary king Tarquinius Priscus (c.616–579 BCE).

> Augustus' great grandfather served in Sicily in the second Punic war as tribune of the soldiers under the command of Aemilius Papus. His grandfather, content with the offices of a municipal town and possessing an abundant income, lived to a peaceful old age.... His own father was the first to become a senator, ... a man of wealth and repute.... He readily attained to high positions and filled them with distinction. (Suetonius, *Deified Augustus* 2–3)

These high positions included a successful governorship of Macedonia, including military victories and rule marked by "equal justice and courage." In section four, Suetonius identifies the distinguished ancestors in Augustus' mother's line. Atia's father descended from a family "displaying many senatorial portraits"[11] and was closely connected "with Pompey the Great." Elsewhere Suetonius notes that the ancestry of Augustus' adopted father, Julius Caesar, derives through Aeneas from Venus (*Deified Julius*, 6). Augustus' standing, power, and prestige are elevated by this ancestry.

Augustus' biological origins, then, embrace a distinguished family of lengthy ancestry. His male ancestors

11. These portraits comprised waxen masks of distinguished ancestors of senatorial rank, which were displayed in the *atrium* of the family residence. Their presence attested the family's distinguished standing.

on both his father's and mother's lines have distinguished themselves in civic service, military success, and political office. These accomplishments are traditional arenas for displays of elite masculine dominance and power. Being positioned in this line augments Augustus' standing.

An interesting feature in Suetonius' narration of Augustus' ancestry highlights the importance of distinguished biological origins in establishing Augustus' greatness and dominance. Three times Suetonius refutes disparaging comments about Augustus' ancestors and origin aimed at diminishing Augustus' standing. So Suetonius reports Augustus' archrival Mark Antony attacking Augustus' great-grandfather and grandfather:

> Marcus Antonius taunts him with his great-grandfather, saying that he was a freedman and a rope-maker from the country about Thurii, while his grandfather was a money-changer. (Suetonius *Deified Augustus* 2)

Such occupations were not honorable for elite men. And concerning Augustus' father, Suetonius reports some opponents attacking his character and identity:

> His father Gaius Octavius was from the beginning of his life a man of wealth and repute, and I cannot but wonder that some have said that he too was a money-changer, and was even employed to distribute bribes at the elections and perform other services in the Campus; for as a matter of fact, being brought up in affluence, he readily attained to high positions and filled them with distinction. (Suetonius, *Deified Augustus* 2)

And concerning Atia's family, Suetonius reports more of Mark Antony's criticism. Antony disparages Augustus for:

having a great-grandfather of African birth, who
kept first a perfumery shop and then a bakery
at Aricia. Cassius of Parma also taunts Augustus
with being the grandson both of a baker and of
a money-changer.

Antony tries to discredit Augustus by attacking aspects of his origin, namely ethnicity and social status, claiming an African, a freedman (former slave), and lower status artisans in his ancestry. Elites did not usually participate in such occupations. Antony's attack is intended to show that Augustus is nothing special and to counter claims of his prestigious origins involving adoption, divine begetting, and distinguished biological descent.

PRESTIGIOUS ORIGINS FOR ELITE MEN

These three forms of origin—adoption, divine begetting, distinguished biological descent—were, in various combinations, commonly attributed to elite figures and national heroes.[12]

For example, centuries before the first century CE, Alexander "the Great," born in 356 BCE, had distinguished biological descent as the son of King Philip II of Macedonia. Traditions also attested his divine origins. He was said to descend from the superhero and strongman Heracles, son of the supreme god Zeus, as well as Achilles, the military hero of the Trojan wars (Diodorus Siculus, *Historica* 17.1.5). A further tradition asserted his divine conception. A serpent was seen lying next to Olympias, Alexander's mother. Her husband Philip stopped having sex with her because he thought that her partner had been a divine

12. On Romulus, Dionysius of Halicarnassus, *Roman Antiquities*, 1.76.3–78.5; Plutarch, *Romulus* 2.3–6; 3.1–3.

Origins

being. The claim was that Alexander's conception involved divine intervention (Plutarch, *Life of Alexander* 2.1—3.2).

Centuries later, in 68 CE, close to the time of the writing of the Gospels, the Julio-Claudian line of Roman emperors descended from Augustus ended when Nero committed suicide in June 68 CE. The new, short-lived emperor Galba could not claim descent from this line of emperors that had spanned some one hundred years. Instead, Suetonius identifies a double and distinguished ancestry for the new emperor, Galba, notably from the god Jupiter and from a distinguished line of ancestors involving both his father and mother.

> Nero was succeeded by Galba, who was related in no degree to the house of the Caesars, although unquestionably of noble origin and of an old and powerful family; for he always added to the inscriptions on his statues that he was the great-grandson of Quintus Catulus Capitolinus, and when he became emperor he even displayed a family tree in his hall in which he carried back his ancestry on his father's side to Jupiter and on his mother's to Pasiphae, the wife of Minos.[13] (Suetonius, *Galba* 2; also Silius Italicus, *Punica* 8.470-71)

How Jupiter brought forth this line is left in mystery. Suetonius continues in the next section of his biography to detail Galba's ancestry comprising "illustrious ancestors and the honorary inscriptions of the entire race." One distinguished ancestor was a consul and orator. Others were warriors. Galba's grandfather was a scholar and writer. His father was a politician who also gained status through

---

13. Pasiphae was the daughter of Helios, the Titan god of the sun. She was married to Minos, king of Crete and son of Zeus/Jupiter; Wiseman, "Legendary Genealogies," 156.

several marriages with women from distinguished families (Suetonius, *Galba* 3).

Subsequently in 81 CE Domitian becomes emperor. A tradition attests that he was the son of Athena/Minerva, the goddess of war and daughter of Zeus. A man tells Apollonius of Tyana that he was under indictment for not recognizing Domitian's divine ancestry.

> ... when sacrificing in Tarentum, where he was a magistrate, he had not added to the public prayers the fact that Domitian was the son of Athena. "You," said Apollonius, "thought that Athena could not have children as a perpetual virgin, but you seem to have forgotten that this goddess once gave birth to a snake for the Athenians." (Philostratus, *Life of Apollonius* 7.24)

How such begetting by the deity Athena/Mercury occurred is again not specified. Of course, in addition to this claim of divine begetting, it was well known that Domitian had elevated human ancestors. His father, the deified Vespasian (69–79 CE), as well as his brother, the deified Titus (79–81 CE), were emperors rendering Domitian the brother and son of a god. Different claims of distinguished origin are complementary.

Other prominent figures were understood to have distinguished ancient ancestors. Suetonius attributes a lengthy genealogy to the Emperor Tiberius dating back to the founding of the city Rome and "the kingly power with Romulus" and marked by distinguished service: "twenty-eight consulships, five dictatorships, seven censorships, six triumphs, and two ovations" (Suetonius, *Tiberius* 1). In his biography of his father-in-law Agricola, governor of Britain, Tacitus introduces Agricola's ancestors, especially his grandfathers, who were "procurators of Caesar," his father, who was a senator, and his mother, who was reputed to be virtuous (*Agricola* 4). The Jewish historian Josephus opens his autobiography by narrating his distinguished ancestry comprising both chief priests and kings (*Life* 1–8).

ORIGINS DISPLAYED

Origins are not only displayed in the genre of ancient biographies. In Athens, a funerary monument honors a very elite figure called Philopappos, a Roman consul, Athenian archon, a king, and a god.[14]

The monument is a two-level structure and was constructed around 115 CE. The first level depicts the greatest accomplishment of Philopappos' career, his inauguration in Rome in 109 CE as consul, the highest Roman magistracy. He is dressed in a Roman tunic and toga. He also wears a rayed crown, a display of his divine ancestry, which the upper level clarifies.

The upper level comprises three sections. In the middle is a statue of Philopappos. On the left is his grandfather, Antiochus IV, the last reigning king of the small Kingdom of Commagene, located between Cappadocia and Syria, west of the Euphrates river. Rome had annexed Commagene in 72 CE. The Emperor Trajan appointed Philopappos to the Senate and in 109 CE he was appointed consul in Rome. Subsequently in Athens he attained the highest honorary rank of *archon*. On the right side is another distinguished figure, Seleucus Nicator, founder of the Seleucid empire and dynasty, with whom Philopappos claimed kinship.

In addition to celebrating Philopappos' exalted political and public accomplishments and attesting his multifaceted identities embracing his Commagenean,

---

14. Miles, "Communicating Culture," 29–36.

Roman, and Athenian connections, the monument also displays his origins.

As is typical of great men, he has human and divine origins. His human origins are most clearly evident in his descent from his grandfather, Antiochus IV, the last reigning king of the small Kingdom of Commagene annexed by Rome in 72 CE. This descent also attests his divinity. As king, his grandfather was considered a god. The lower level of the monument presents Philopappos in his chariot wearing a rayed crown, which signifies his divinity.

The statue of Seleucus Nicator suggests another claim to divinity. After Seleucus Nicator's death (281 BCE), his son and successor Antiochus I initiated a

> cult for his continual honoring as Zeus Nicator. Linking Philopappos with Seleucus Nicator associates him with Zeus/Jupiter.

Less illustrious ancestors?

Some genealogies, however, did not hesitate to include less illustrious ancestors. Suetonius recognizes that the Emperor Tiberius' ancestors included those who performed "many distinguished services" as well as those "of the opposite character." These negative characters that Suetonius mentions include a sexual predator, one who tried to grab power, and a military commander who ignored the auspices and launched and lost a naval battle. Suetonius generalizes the family's faults as despising common folks and being "headstrong and stubborn" (*Tiberius* 2).

Likewise, Suetonius remarks that Emperor "Nero degenerated from the good qualities of his ancestors, yet he reproduced the vices of each of them." Suetonius narrates the actions of numerous villainous ancestors, ending with a comment from Nero's father concerning the newborn Nero that portended his future character and actions: "nothing that was not abominable and a public bane could be born of Agrippina and himself" (Suetonius, *Nero* 2–6).

Suetonius introduces the Emperor Vespasian's family as "obscure and without family portraits," yet not one of which "to be ashamed" (*Deified Vespasian* 1). The family comprised tax-collectors and bankers. It also included some with military and political service, including one who fought on Pompey's side but fled the battlefield. Suetonius reports claims that a family member was a contractor for the day-labourers who tilled fields, but he declares he has found no evidence for this claim. Subsequently, Suetonius says that Vespasian "never tried to conceal his former lowly condition but often paraded it." He laughed at those who tried to associate his family origins with Hercules (Suetonius, *Deified Vespasian* 12).[15]

THE GOSPELS

The Roman world commonly constructed the identity of great men by setting forth a man's origins in multiple terms: divine action, distinguished genealogy, adoption, and biological ancestors with illustrious accomplishments. Not surprisingly, the Gospels employ similar strategies of genealogy, divine action, adoption, and ancestry in constructing Jesus' identity. What arises in the intersectionality between Roman constructions of male greatness and the Gospel's construction of Jesus' identity?

The Gospels reinscribe or imitate, as well as depart from, these strategies in constructing Jesus' identity by various combinations of genealogy, divine action, adoption, and human ancestors. These strategies construct Jesus' greatness not in terms of military and political accomplishments but in terms of his commission to perform God's empire. God, not the gods nor Rome, constitutes his greatness through conception, distinguished ancestors, and adoption, yet his parents are not of distinguished standing but of low status and occupation.

Jesus: genealogies, ancestors, conceived by the divine Spirit

Two of the Gospels—Matthew and Luke—employ genealogies in constructing Jesus' character.

15. Hekster, "Descendants of God."

Origins

Matthew's Gospel

Matthew's Gospel opens with Jesus' genealogy (1:2–17).[16] Its structure is patriarchal and threefold, involving thirty-nine uses of the formula "A was the father of B" (1:17). It traces a line of male ancestors from the esteemed Abraham to the honored king David (1:2–6a), through a line of kings to the tragedy of exile in Babylon and return to the land (1:6b–12a), to Mary's delivery of Jesus (1:12b–16).

The Gospel's opening verse identifies Jesus as descendent of two of the dominant men in Israel's national narrative, Abraham and David (1:1). The genealogy's structure continues to place Jesus in relation to these heroes. Through the people's legendary founder Abraham, God had promised to bless all the people of the earth (cf. Gen 12:3) thereby positioning the nation at the center of the world. Jesus' ancestors also include those who had attained the highest political office in the land. To David, king of the united people, God had promised a line of kings and a kingdom that would last forever (2 Sam 7:12–14a). And God had entrusted to David as king the task of representing God's justice and purposes among the people (Pss 2; 72). The genealogy sets Jesus in the company of and as the heir to these high-profile national figures who exercised defining roles in Israel's identity and traditions.

As with the genealogies of Tiberius and Nero, this genealogy also sets Jesus in company that is not illustrious. David's record as an adulterer and murderer is hardly stellar. Other kings mentioned in verses 6–11 were not faithful. Solomon, Abijah, Joram, Ahaz, and Manasseh are evaluated negatively in the tradition for not ruling according to the divine purposes. The inclusion of five women is unusual but not unique. One of the five, Rahab, was a Canaanite

16. Carter, *Matthew and the Margins*, 53–66.

prostitute who is commended for protecting Joshua's spies in Jericho (Josh 2). The exile event is interpreted in some texts as divine punishment on a sinful people who have failed to live faithfully (2 Kgs 24:16). Most of the eleven names listed in verses 11–15 are so inconsequential that they do not appear elsewhere in the tradition. And the genealogy ends with a reference to Jesus' birth from Mary who had become pregnant as an unmarried though betrothed virgin, and is now married to Joseph, a small-town, lower-status, wood-working artisan (1:20; 13:55).

Yet throughout these mixed circumstances, the genealogy assumes, though it does not name, the presence and purposes of God manifested in these human lives and circumstances. Those purposes include universal blessing (Abraham), justice (David), and judgment (exile). Jesus is set in the narrative of divinely sanctioned characters and events that enact the divine will. Subsequent verses will name this will as manifesting God's saving presence and empire in the midst of Rome's empire (1:21–23; 4:17).

The wording of verse 16, "Mary of whom Jesus was born," is elaborated in verses 18–25. Four times these verses attribute Jesus' conception not to Joseph but to the divine Spirit. Mary is pregnant when she and Joseph have not had sex (1:18, 25). She is pregnant by the Holy Spirit (1:18, 20). An angel sent from God declares the Spirit's role in Jesus' conception.

And in 1:25, Joseph, son of David (1:20), adopts Jesus by naming him. Subsequently, in an adoptive act, God declares Jesus to be "my son" (3:17).

Luke's Gospel

Unlike Matthew's Gospel, Luke's Gospel does not open with a genealogy. Rather, with reference to Jesus, Luke's Gospel opens with his conception story. As with Matthew, an angel sent from God makes the announcement though not to Joseph but to Mary. She will conceive a child by the Spirit who will be called son of God (Luke 1:28–35). This child is located in line with the illustrious ancestor David (1:32) and Abraham (1:55).

Moreover, in addition to this divine conception account (also 2:49; 3:23?), the Gospel affirms Joseph as Jesus' father. In 2:27 and 2:48, "his parents" (plural!) and "his father" bring Jesus to the temple. At 4:22, the synagogue names Jesus as "Joseph's son." The identification of Joseph's fatherhood indicates either a biological or adoptive act.

In addition, Luke's Gospel employs a genealogy just after God has adopted Jesus as God's son at Jesus' baptism (Luke 3:21–22) and before Jesus' public ministry begins in verse fourteen of chapter 4 (Luke 3:23–38). Unlike Matthew's genealogy, which works forward from Abraham to Joseph, Luke's genealogy begins with Joseph (3:23) and works back to Adam "son of God" (3:38). Both gospels trace Jesus' line through Joseph. There is further agreement in the section linking Abraham to David in which Luke 3:31–34 shares twelve names with Matt 1:2–6. Yet the two genealogies also have significantly different content. Verses 23–31 (Jesus to David) share only five names with Matthew's genealogy and verses 34–38 (Abraham to Adam) have no parallel. Not only do the two genealogies not share a three-part structure, Luke identifies seventy-six names while Matthew features forty-two.

Like Matthew, Luke's genealogy links Jesus with Abraham and David, though they are not highlighted as in Matthew's structuring. More important is that Luke's genealogy pushes past Abraham to Adam "son of God," the primal human being representative of all humans. This identification reinforces Jesus' origin from and connection to God. It emphasizes Jesus' identity as God's son or agent in conception and adopted in baptism, legitimated by God at the outset of Jesus' public missional activity, anointed by "the Spirit of the Lord . . . to bring good news to the poor, . . . to proclaim release to the captives and recovery of sight to the blind, to let the oppressed go free, to proclaim the year of the Lord's favor" (Luke 4:18–19). Luke's use of these multiple claims of origin—divine conception, biological descent/adoption by Joseph, a link to God via Adam, distinguished ancestors—mirrors, in Kochenash's view, claims about Augustus: "being fathered by Apollo . . . descent from Aeneas—through adoption by Julius—who was said to have been the offspring of Aphrodite/Venus."[17]

These significant differences between the two genealogies underscore that they are not primarily offering historical data. Nor can they be reconciled. More important is to understand their function in relation to the Greco-Roman biographies discussed above. This intersectionality constructs Jesus' identity as a great man, defined by divine origin, adoption, and association with distinguished ancestors. Jesus derives greatness and dominance from these actions and associations.

Mark's Gospel

Mark's Gospel does not employ a genealogy for Jesus. Rather, the Gospel presents Jesus' baptism as his adoption by God.[18] Mark's three-verse scene occurs before Jesus' public activity begins (1:9–11). Verse 9 sets the scene of John's baptism of Jesus. Verse 10 describes Jesus ascending from the water, the heavens opening, and the Spirit descending "like

---

17. Kochenash, *Roman Self-Representation*, 33.
18. Peppard, *Son of God,* 106–31; Carter, *Mark*, 10–13.

a dove" on Jesus. Verse 11 presents a voice (God) speaking from heaven.

God addresses Jesus as "my son," denoting God's adoption of Jesus. Previously God had adopted Israel into a father-son covenant relationship, which bestowed a new status and identity (Exod 4:22–23; Hos 11:1–4). God had adopted Israel's kings as sons or agents of the divine purposes (2 Sam 7:5–17; Ps 2:7). The Spirit's descent "as a dove" into Jesus frames Jesus' life from the outset as an expression of God's will and constitutes Jesus' identity as the adopted son or agent empowered to perform the divine purposes. Interestingly, a sign of doves nesting in a palm tree persuaded Julius Caesar to adopt Augustus as his son, heir, and successor (Suetonius *Aug* 94.11). God declares Jesus to be the one God has chosen: "you are my son, my beloved, you I have chosen."[19]

Yet also, existing alongside this divine adoption, the Gospel recognizes Jesus' biological origins. In Mark 6:1–6, Jesus' teaching in a synagogue brings a response from the audience. They wonder about the source of his teaching and actions, speculating, "Is not this the carpenter, the son of Mary . . ." with four named brothers and at least two unnamed sisters (also 3:32).[20] Joseph is not named anywhere in Mark's Gospel,[21] though it would be incorrect to assume that identifying Jesus in relation to his mother is a slur. As I noted in the previous chapter, the Greek word translated "carpenter" (*tektōn*) indicates a craftsman working on "roof

19. The common translation is, "with you I am well-pleased." But the verb *eudokēsa* is better translated as "chosen," or "selected" (1 Cor 1:21; Gal 1:15).

20. Carter, *Mark*, 143–47.

21. Luke's version of the scene explicitly names Joseph (Luke 4:22). Matthew's scene identifies Jesus as "the son of the carpenter" (Matt 13:55) as well as explicitly naming Joseph as Mary's husband (1:16–24; 2:13, 19).

structures . . . oil mills, furniture, wagons, chariots wheels, . . . barges, boats, . . . water wheels, . . . wooden doors and windows, . . . towers, storage facilities, military defense walls, bridges, siege machines."[22] Some artisans did quite well economically. The presentation of Jesus as an artisan constructs him to be a person of very modest origins. This is the same person that the Gospel presents as the chosen by God as God's agent or son.

John's Gospel

John's Gospel similarly combines Jesus' humble biological origins with divine origins. Twice Jesus is identified as "son of Joseph" (John 1:45; 6:42) though without identifying the occupation of carpenter. Both Jesus and Joseph are linked to the small village of Nazareth, which Nathanael disparages as not producing any significant person (1:45–46). Jesus' mother appears in several scenes (2:1–12; 6:42; 19:25–27). The Gospel, though, does not offer a genealogy nor narrate any miraculous action by the Spirit in causing Jesus' conception, as do Matthew and Luke.[23] Jesus is one of the common folks in Galilee.

Yet pervasive is the Gospel's repeated construction of Jesus as "the son" and "the son of God." Repeatedly the Gospel constructs God as the Father of Jesus and Jesus is said to originate "in the beginning" with God (1:1–3). He is constructed as coming from heaven (3:13), from the Father (10:18), from God (6:46). This language of his origin affirms Jesus' close relationship with God and his identity as the agent sanctioned by God to reveal God's purposes. His origin with God and from God authorizes and legitimizes his words and actions as representative of God's will

22. Huebner, *Papyri*, 66, also 65–86.
23. John's Jesus has brothers: 2:12; 7:3–5, 10.

in the midst of Rome's empire. The Gospel, though, does not specify how this origin with God came about.

CONCLUSION

What does the intertextuality between Roman attention to origins of dominant and powerful men and the Gospels' construction of Jesus' origins display?

We have established how important were claims of the origins of an important man in the Roman Empire. Genealogies, divine origins, adoption, and distinguished biological ancestors constructed emperors as distinguished, powerful men, agents of Roman domination and representatives of the gods. The Gospels use similar means to construct Jesus' origins: distinguished genealogies, divine origin, adoption by God. Intertextuality with "the Roman mentality to venerate benefactors by ascribing" divine origins to them means that "a divine origin was appropriate for the chief benefactor and founder" of the Jesus-movement.[24]

But there are some differences. The Matthean and Lukan genealogies set Jesus in relation to God's interactions with Israel and to distinguished and anonymous ancestors, not in relation to Rome. Accounts of divine workings in his conception and adoption emphasize Jesus' commission to manifest the divine purposes and empire. These accounts of his origins authorize Jesus, empowering and legitimizing his activity on behalf of God, at times imitative and at times contestive, in the midst of Rome's empire. Yet as with several emperors, Jesus too has ancestors who were less than accomplished and virtuous. And his parents are non-elite folks, with his father an artisan carpenter. Jesus is one of the common people commissioned by God to manifest God's empire in the midst of Rome's empire.

---

24. Talbert, "Miraculous Conceptions," 85.

DISCUSSION QUESTIONS

1. What role do stories about the circumstances of your origins play in constructing your identity?

2. How did eminent Roman figures like the Emperor Augustus or the Athenian Philopappos utilize accounts of their origins to establish their greatness?

3. What claims of origin do the Gospels of Matthew and of Luke employ in constructing Jesus' identity?

4. What claims of origin do the Gospels of Mark and of John employ in constructing Jesus' identity?

5. In constructing Jesus' identity, how are the Gospels similar to and different from claims made about important men in the Roman Empire?

4

PORTENTS OF GREATNESS

THE ACCOUNTS OF THE birth of Jesus in the Gospels of Matthew and Luke include distinctive features: prophecies of future greatness; dreams; unusual characters (magi); a mobile star; an endangered child; a wonder-child. These features are common in narratives of the births of famous men in the Roman world. Intertextuality between the features of Jesus' birth and dominant Roman men establishes Jesus among the great imperial men, yet redefined as a ruler and agent of divine, not Roman, purposes.

PROPHECIES OF FUTURE GREATNESS

The Gospels of Matthew and Luke include scenes in which Joseph in Matthew's Gospel and Mary in Luke's Gospel experience dreams in which "angels of the Lord" declare to them Jesus' future greatness.

An angel appears to Matthew's Joseph in a dream after he has decided to divorce the pregnant Mary. The angel instructs him not to do so because Mary has not been unfaithful. The child is conceived through the Holy Spirit. The angel instructs Joseph to name the baby "Jesus," and explains the name's choice. The name's meaning declares Jesus' future mission, "for he will save his people from their sins" (Matt 1:21). The people's sins, particularly the leaders who had crucified Jesus, had been punished when Rome destroyed Jerusalem and its temple in 70 CE. In this post-70 Gospel, the angel announces Jesus' commission to save the people from Rome's punishing sovereignty and presence.

Subsequently, angels appear in dreams to protect the subject of this prophecy of future greatness. In a dream, "an angel of the Lord appeared to Joseph" to warn him of Herod's murderous plans against Jesus. The angel directs Joseph, Mary, and Jesus to flee to Egypt (Matt 2:13). After Herod's death, an angel of the Lord again appears to Joseph and directs their return to Israel and Galilee (Matt 2:19–20). Though not mentioning an angel, a further dream directs them to Nazareth to escape the dangerous king Archelaus, the son of king Herod (Matt 2:22).

Luke's Mary receives a visit from an angel though it is not specified if it was in a dream. The angel informs her she will become pregnant and declares Jesus' future greatness.

> He will be great, and will be called the Son of the Most High, and the Lord God will give to him the throne of his ancestor David. He will reign over the house of Jacob forever, and of his kingdom there will be no end. (Luke 1:32–33)

This declaration of Jesus' future greatness recognizes Jesus' agency on behalf of God as "Son of the Most High." His greatness centers on his identity as king in the line of King David and his task forever is to rule Israel as representative of the divine will.

The angel's prediction is confirmed subsequently. An angel declares to shepherds that the newborn Jesus is "a Savior, who is the Messiah, the Lord" (Luke 2:11). When Joseph and Mary bring the infant Jesus to the temple, they encounter Simeon who has been waiting for the "Lord's Messiah." On seeing Jesus he declares him to represent God's salvation for all people, "a light for revelation to the Gentiles and for glory to your people Israel" (Luke 2:25–32). Subsequently the elderly widow Anna speaks about Jesus "to all who were looking for the redemption of Jerusalem" from Roman domination (Luke 2:36–38).

ROMAN FIGURES

These declarations of Jesus' future greatness create intertextuality with a similar Roman practice whereby predictions of future greatness construct various elite Roman (male) figures. Aeneas in Virgil's *Aeneid* is divinely commissioned and guided in his journey from a destroyed Troy to Italy to found Rome. Looking down on the Trojans swept onto the shore of Libya, Jupiter, ruler of "the world of men and gods," responds to his daughter Venus' concerns about her son Aeneas by naming Rome's glorious future of ruling "sea and all lands" (*Aeneid* 1.236) in which Aeneas plays a central role. Aeneas will

> wage a great war in Italy, shall crush proud nations and for his people shall set up laws and city walls; . . . for these I set no bounds in space and time but have given empire without end, . . . lords of the world and the nation of the toga. Thus it is decreed. (*Aeneid* 1.261–64, 278–79, 282).

Later in Book 6, Aeneas visits his dead father in Hades. Anchises reminds Aeneas of his destiny to rule the world with restraint and benefits among the cooperative ("peace with justice") and with crushing force among the resistant:

> "You, Roman, be sure to rule the world, . . . to crown peace with justice, to spare the vanquished, and to crush the proud." (*Aeneid* 6.851–53)

Jupiter's prediction in Book 1 does not concern only Aeneas; it extends across Roman history to the Emperor Augustus. Jupiter predicts Augustus' future greatness, first as an earthly ruler who advances Rome's empire across oceans and second as a great and dominant man who will be elevated to heaven as a god.

> From this noble line shall be born the Trojan Caesar (Augustus) who shall extend his empire to the ocean, his glory to the stars, a Julius, name descended from the great Iulus! Him, in days to come, shall you (Venus), anxious no more, welcome to heaven, laden with Eastern spoils; he, too, shall be invoked in vows. (*Aeneid* 1.286–90)

The link between Aeneas and Augustus is secured at the end of book eight (8.626–731) with Vulcan fashioning a shield for Aeneas that displays the battle of Actium of September 31 BCE in which Octavian-Augustus defeats Antony and Cleopatra, thereby clearing the way for Augustus to gain supreme power as emperor.

Among descriptions of various omens signaling Augustus' birth, Suetonius narrates several declarations of Augustus' future greatness (*Deified Augustus* 94). At Augustus' birth, a senator Publius Nigidius declares to Augustus' father "that the ruler of the world had been born."[1] In Thrace, Augustus' father consulted priests at an altar and

---

1. A physiognomist declares that the young Titus will become emperor (Suetonius, *Deified Titus* 2).

they made the same prediction that his baby would rule the world after witnessing wine poured on the altar transforming into a huge pillar of fire. The last time such a fiery event had happened involved the world-ruling Alexander the Great. Augustus' father also has a dream in which his son appears to him as Jupiter Optimus Maximus, ruler of the world. Quintus Catulus dreamed of the young Augustus "in the lap of Jupiter" and Jupiter announced that "the boy was being reared to be the saviour of his country" (Suetonius, *Deified Augustus* 94.5–8).

Predictions of future greatness, often associated with conception and birth but also emerging in adult life, provided divine sanction and legitimation for the accomplishments and (commonly) political domination of a ruler. The declarations concerning Jesus' future greatness as a king and savior in accord with the disclosed divine purposes construct him as a great man.

DREAMS

Dreams play an important role in these last two instances of predictions concerning Augustus' future greatness. While attitudes to dreams varied across the Roman Empire and some were skeptical,[2] others understood dreams to be means of communication or revelation from gods through lower divine beings (*daimons*; angels) to humans concerning the world's future, the significance of key people, and the will of the gods.[3] As with Matthew's Gospel, dreams occur in narratives of the conceptions and births of powerful men to portend their future greatness. Given that the narratives look back on the careers of major political and

2. Harris, "Roman Opinions," 27–31.

3. Dodson, *Reading Dreams*, 12–13; Litwa, *How the Gospels*, 96–97.

military figures, we can note that twenty-twenty hindsight proves useful in evaluating the veracity or reliability of a dream.

Plutarch narrates dreams associated with the conception of Alexander the Great (*Alexander* 2.2–4). His mother Olympias dreamed that a lightning bolt struck her womb and kindled a great fire. His father Philip dreamed that he sealed his wife's womb with the image of a lion. He saw a snake sleeping near his wife and interpreted it to be a divine being involved in his son's conception. These dreams "function to portend the future greatness and distinction of the unborn child."[4]

Suetonius employs dreams, sometimes associated with birth, sometimes associated with adult life, to signal greatness. The adult Julius Caesar, concerned that his life had accomplished nothing in comparison with Alexander the Great's accomplishments, dreams that he "was destined to rule the world" (Suetonius, *Deified Julius* 7.2). Suetonius declares that Augustus "was not indifferent to" various dreams, both his own and that of others, that portended his future greatness (Suetonius, *Deified Augustus* 91.1–2). Both his mother Atia and his father Octavius had dreams about Augustus' conception involving Apollo's involvement. These dreams, and those of his father and Quintus Catulus noted above, portended "his future greatness and uninterrupted good fortune" (Suetonius, *Deified Augustus* 91.1).

The adult Galba, emperor for seven months between June 68 CE and January 69 CE, dreams that Fortune was prompting him to action (Suetonius, *Galba* 4.3). A priest of Jupiter, prompted by a dream, found written verses predicting that "there would come forth from Spain the ruler and lord of the world" (*Galba* 9.2). Vespasian dreams that "the beginning of good fortune for himself and his family"

4. Dodson, *Reading Dreams*, 107.

would follow after Nero had a tooth extracted, an event that happened the next day (Suetonius, *Deified Vespasian* 5.5). And a dream involving scales or balances that showed he and his sons ruled for the same length of time as Claudius and Nero celebrates his dynastic rule (*Deified Vespasian* 25).[5]

Through dreams, gods communicated with humans, identifying and commissioning great men to exercise dominating power, predicting the future, shaping the world. So it is for Matthew's and Luke's Jesus.

OMENS AND PORTENTS

In addition to predictions of future greatness and dreams, unusual happenings associated with powerful figures portended their future greatness.

Suetonius introduces "an account of the omens" accompanying Augustus' birth and afterwards "from which it was possible to anticipate and perceive his future greatness and uninterrupted good fortune" (Suetonius, *Deified Augustus* 94.1). Some of the signs (Atia's conception; dreams; Publius Nigidius' prediction; the priests of Thrace; the dreams of Quintus Catullus; 94.4–8) have been mentioned above. Suetonius adds the following portents:

- In Velitrae, the town of Augustus' father, lightning struck a town wall that was interpreted to indicate a citizen of the town (Augustus) would rule the world.

- In response to a portent predicting the birth of a king for the Roman people, the senate decreed all male children should be killed, but those with pregnant wives ensured the decree was not filed and so annulled it thereby ensuring Augustus' survival.

5. Dodson, *Reading Dreams,* 112–15.

- The infant Augustus is placed in his cradle in the evening; in the morning he is found lying on a tower facing the rising sun.
- The young Augustus successfully commands frogs to be silent.
- While he was eating lunch, an eagle snatched bread from his hand, soared high, and then returned to replace the bread.
- A dream links Jupiter and Augustus.
- His senatorial tunic was ripped and fell at his feet, which some interpreted to signify that the senate "would one day be brought to his feet."
- Julius Caesar decided not to cut down a palm tree, from which sprang forth a shoot that grew very quickly and was bigger than the palm tree. Birds nested in it and caused Caesar to adopt Augustus as his heir and successor as ruler.
- Augustus' horoscope attested his greatness so Augustus made his birth under the sign of Capricornus known by means of a stamped coin.

Such signs or omens pointed to Augustus' greatness. While they enabled Augustus to "perceive his future greatness and uninterrupted good fortune," equally important was that they made others aware that Augustus was chosen by the gods and destined for great power.

VESPASIAN

Suetonius records a similar list of portents by which Vespasian "began to cherish the hope of imperial dignity" (*Deified Vespasian* 5) and by which others came to perceive his destiny as emperor (69–79 CE).

Portents of Greatness

- An impressive tree portended great success for a grandchild "who would be a Caesar."
- Young Vespasian failed in his office as aedile, a lower-rank elected position with responsibility for caring for the city's infrastructure including cleaning the streets. The Emperor Gaius Caligula punished him by heaping mud into his toga. Some interpreted this act as an omen that one day his country would come under his protection.
- During breakfast, a dog brought a severed hand to him. The hand symbolized the power he was to exercise.
- An ox burst into Vespasian's dining room, fell at Vespasian's feet, and bowed his neck. The omen signified Vespasian's great power before which even animals voluntarily submit.
- A tree on his grandfather's farm was suddenly torn up without a storm. The next day it grew upright even more strongly.
- An oracle from Mount Carmel in Judea promised him success in whatever he desired.
- Josephus, a high-status Jewish priest and military commander captured by Vespasian, declares Vespasian would become emperor.
- The Emperor Nero dreamed that he was to take the chariot of Jupiter Optimus Maximus to Vespasian's house, thereby recognizing him as Nero's successor.
- A statue of the Deified Julius Caesar turned to the east where Vespasian was waging war in Judea and where legions proclaimed Vespasian emperor.

- Before a battle at Betriacum, two eagles fought. A third eagle came from the east and drove off the victor. The battle at Betriacum was fought between two imperial claimants, Otho and Vitellius, with the latter the winner. Vitellius was emperor from April to December 69 CE. The third eagle represented Vespasian, whose troops in the east had hailed him as emperor and subsequently killed Vitellius. Vespasian ruled from late 69 CE till his death in 79 CE.

Such omens signified Vespasian's "imperial dignity" both for him and for others, thereby augmenting his authority as emperor.

MATTHEW'S GOSPEL

In Matthew's Gospel, omens mark Jesus' birth and portend his future greatness, not as emperor but as king in the line of David and as representative of the liberative divine purposes in the midst of Rome's empire. The Matthean portents include magi ("wise men from the east"); a mobile star; ancient texts; and angels and dreams.

Magi

Magi—neither "wise men" nor "kings"—frequently functioned as political advisers. They used multiple identities and functions as astrologers, legates, intellectuals, and priests to perform their roles. They interpreted dreams and natural and heavenly phenomena like stars as well as performing rituals to secure divine favor and advice for the well-being of the kings and empires they served (Strabo, 15.1.68). Accordingly, as members of the Babylonian and Persian priestly class, they had access to and advice for ruling powers, as the magi do in approaching Herod in Matt 2:2–3.

At Cyrus' birth, magi played a key role in interpreting King Astyages' dream that Cyrus would be king (Herodotus 1.107–30, esp. 107–8). They interpreted an eclipse of the sun as a favorable sign for the Persian ruler Xerxes to attack Greek cities (Herodotus 7.37). They interpret the night in which Alexander was born and the temple of Diana burned in Ephesus as the birth of "Asia's deadly curse" (Cicero, *De Divinatione* 1.23.47). In Dan 2:1–10, they serve the Babylonian ruler Nebuchadnezzar, who demands that they tell him his dream and its interpretation.

The Roman proconsul of Cyprus Sergius Paulus (46–48 CE) had a Jewish magus named Bar-Jesus or Elymas as an advisor (Acts 13:6–8). The Emperor Nero received the Parthian-sponsored Armenian King Tiridates and his entourage, which included magi, who initiated Nero into their sacred banquets (Pliny, *NH* 30.6.16–17). Nero uses "rites performed by Magi, in the effort to summon [his dead mother's] shade" and to seek forgiveness after he had her put to death (Suetonius, *Nero* 34.4).

While their identity as political servants is clear, magi could also be subversive. For example, led by Gaumata the magus, they rebelled against, and replaced, the Achaemenid King Cambyses. Pliny notes the magi "objected to Nero" and Pliny dismisses their magic as "detestable, vain, and idle" (*NH* 30.6.16–17). Seneca mocks astrologers who had been predicting the Emperor Claudius' death "every year every month" (*Apocolocyntosis* 3.2). The magi in Matthew subvert Herod's power by paying homage to an unsanctioned king, Jesus, and not offering homage to Herod. They defy Herod by refusing to be his spies and not returning to Jerusalem to report on Jesus' whereabouts (Matt 2:12–13a).

The introduction of the magi characters signals the international and imperial-political stage for the significance of Jesus' birth. The scene evokes and imitates trappings of imperial and kingly power, directing attention to Jesus' importance, while simultaneously contesting imperial claims since these magi bear witness to a king who is sanctioned by Israel's God and not by Rome, and whom Herod experiences as a threat (Matt 2:3).

The magi follow a star

Magi interpret astrological signs. Stars and heavenly phenomena portending subsequent great success are linked with the births of Emperors Augustus (Suetonius, *Augustus* 94.2), Tiberius (Suetonius, *Tiberius* 14.2), and Nero (Dio Cassius 61.2.1–4). It was widely believed, though dismissed by Pliny, that stars brightened at the birth of a special person (Pliny, *NH* 2.28).

Stars underscored special events. Virgil narrates that a star persuaded Anchises to leave burning Troy with his son Aeneas, a journey that would lead to Aeneas' founding of Rome (Virgil, *Aeneid* 2.692–704). Suetonius attests the active interest of various emperors in astrology: Tiberius was "addicted to astrology" (*Tiberius* 14; 69). Also attentive to astrologers were Emperors Gaius Caligula (*Gaius Caligula* 19; 45; 57), Nero (*Nero* 6; 36; 40), Vitellius (*Vitellius* 3), Vespasian (*Vespasian* 14, 25), Titus (*Titus* 9), and Domitian (*Domitian* 14; 15; 16). Nero, for example, learns of a comet that was interpreted to portend his death. An astrologer Balbillus teaches him that the omen might be averted by the death of a prominent man, which Suetonius links to his execution of the Piso-led conspirators (Suetonius, *Nero* 36). Suetonius (*Nero* 60) also notes that Nero believed the prediction of astrologers that after misfortunes (reversals of

Roman power in Armenia and Britain) there would be "the restitution of all his former fortunes." Seneca recognizes that "on even the slightest motion of heavenly bodies hang the fortune of nations" (*To Marcian on Consolation*, 18.3). A comet, a star resembling a sword, and other heavenly apparitions marked Rome's destruction of Jerusalem in 70 CE (Josephus, *J.W.* 6.289–98). Several emperors expelled astrologers from Rome because they brought bad news.[6]

The Matthean text does not explain how the magi gained insight into the significance of the star, which they observed "at its rising" and which had led them to Jerusalem (Matt 2:2). Yet when others do not, they travel considerable distance in pursuit of it, recognize it signifies the birth of a king, and discern that homage is an appropriate response. They perceive from the heavenly world that God is at work and has intervened to challenge the imperial world. And they destabilize the Rome-appointed King Herod and his allies by asking a threatening question about a newborn king not sanctioned by Roman power but representing divine purposes (2:1–12).

Matthew's Gospel cites ancient texts

Matthew's narrative marks Jesus' birth by citing ancient texts, which are removed from the ancient contexts that they had addressed previously and are now read in relation to Jesus and continue to underscore his mission

Verse 6 of chapter 2 interprets Jesus' birth in Bethlehem, the town in which Samuel anointed David king (1 Sam 16:1–13). The verse cites Mic 5:2 to interpret Bethlehem as a town from which "shall come a ruler who is to shepherd my people Israel." The ancient text in the name

---

6. Tiberius (Suetonius, *Tiberius* 36); Claudius (Tacitus, *Ann* 12.52); Vitellius (Suetonius, *Vitellius* 14.4).

of the eighth-century BCE Judean prophet Micah did not originally refer to Jesus. But the Gospel interprets it as portending Jesus' greatness as a ruler or shepherd for Israel in the midst of Rome's empire.

Likewise, the Gospel uses another ancient text to interpret the flight of Joseph, Mary, and infant Jesus to safety in Egypt away from Herod's murderous rage. Verse 15 of chapter 2 cites Hos 11:1 from the eighth-century Israelite prophet Hosea. Again, originally, it did not refer to Jesus. Rather the prophet lamented Israel's faithlessness and ingratitude after the liberation from Egyptian slavery. But now the Gospel interprets it in relation to Jesus. The Matthean use of this ancient text links Moses and Jesus, Egyptian rule and Roman dominance, past liberation and the future deliverance that Jesus will accomplish.

The Gospel's third citation of an ancient text performs a similar function. Verse 18 of chapter 2 cites the sixth-century prophet Jeremiah, who was lamenting the grief of those exiled to Babylon (Jer 31:15). Now the Gospel uses the prophet's words from another time and experience to express the lament and weeping of parents after Herod's murderous attack on the infants of Bethlehem. Jeremiah's words had referred to two national disasters at the hands of two imperial powers, namely defeats by the empires of Assyria in 722 BCE and of Babylon in 587 BCE. Yet neither defeat was permanent. God reversed both tragedies, ended the assertion of imperialist power, and released Israel from imperial domination. Citing the prophet Jeremiah creates a parallel with the Gospel's context of submission to Roman rule. It points to another dimension of Jesus' role, namely the future defeat of Roman imperial power.

The citation of these ancient texts creates significant intertextualities with the imperial narratives of Roman power. In the previous discussion, we have noted features of these narratives. In Virgil's *Aeneid*, for example, the narrative of Rome' greatness and world domination begins with the god Jupiter declaring Rome's destiny of worldwide domination (*Aeneid* 1.236, 278–83). This divine decree and sanction lead to the election of Aeneas and begins the long line of ancestors that will result in Caesar Augustus' worldwide rule as emperor (*Aeneid* 1.286–90). Aeneas' destiny to "rule the world . . . to spare the vanquished and to crush the proud" anticipates Augustus' destiny (*Aeneid* 6.851–53) and his victory over Mark Antony at Actium in 31 BCE (*Aeneid* 8.679–98).

The ancient texts featured in Matthew 2 tell a different and contestive story. They foreground a different divine actor, a different chosen human agent (Jesus), a different mission, and a certain outcome of worldwide rule that ends Roman rule.

An endangered child

In Matthew chapter 2, Herod is the Rome-sanctioned king (Josephus, *J.W.* 1.388–93). He is greatly threatened by the sudden, Magi-delivered news of a newborn king of the Jews. Either Rome had withdrawn its sanction from Herod, or he faces an uprising and rebellion from a populist figure. Either way, Herod considers Jesus a rival and seeks to kill him.

The motif of the endangered special child, the future ruler or founder or deliverer, has a long history. The story of the infant Moses, a founder and deliverer of the Israelite people pursued by Pharaoh, is well known (Exod 2:1–10). The motif also has significant intertextuality with Roman traditions.

One such scene involves Rome's legendary founders, Romulus and Remus. Both Jesus and Romulus and Remus are conceived by divine action. The mother of the twins, Rhea Silva, was impregnated by Mars, the war-god. As infants they were endangered by king Amulius, the brother of Numitor, Rhea Silvia's father. Amulius was determined that no descendant of Numitor would rule. He saw Romulus and Remus as rivals and sought to kill them by exposing and/or drowning them. But they survived to be nursed by a she-wolf and grew up as shepherds.[7]

The Emperor Augustus' birth was threatened when an omen in Rome was understood to portend the birth of a king. Refusing to have a king, the Senate decreed that any male child born that year was to be killed. The future Augustus was saved, though, when those whose wives were pregnant did not file the decree and thereby invalidated it (Suetonius, *Deified Augustus* 94.3).

Suetonius styles Tiberius' infancy and youth as marked by "hardship and tribulation" (*Tiberius* 6). The dangers arose from his parents' flight from political rivals to places such as Praeneste, Naples, Sicily, Achaia (where his father joined Mark Antony), and Rome (where he reversed his allegiance and declared loyalty to Augustus). Tiberius' cries as an infant nearly betrayed the family to opponents on several occasions. On another occasion, a forest fire threatened their survival.

Again the intertextuality between the Gospel and these Roman traditions functions to locate Jesus among great men. He is important enough to have opponents and to pose a threat to the ruling powers and their interests. In Matthew's Gospel, his opponent is the Rome-appointed King Herod, the face of Roman power and interests in Judea. Yet the efforts of this Roman-sanctioned king to kill

---

7. Matt 2:6; Dionysius of Halicarnassus, *Roman Antiquities* 1:72–90; 2:1–76; Livy, *History of Rome* Book 1, opening sections; Plutarch, *Life of Romulus*. Shepherds of course feature in Luke 2:8–20.

Jesus is thwarted by divine protection through the interventions of angels and dreams and by the faithful and courageous actions of Joseph and Mary.

A *wunderkind*

While Luke's Gospel does not employ the motif of the child in danger, it does feature a scene of Jesus the wonder child displaying exceptional talent. This scene exists in intertextual relationship with another motif in the accounts of great men, that of the wonder child whose adult-like behaviors display and anticipate future greatness.

At age twelve, Luke's Jesus travels from Galilee to Jerusalem for the Passover festival. After the festival, while his parents return to Galilee, Jesus stays in Jerusalem, in the temple, where, three days later, his parents find him in debate with the leading teachers or interpreters of the traditions. He was

> sitting among the teachers, listening to them and asking them questions. And all who heard him were amazed at his understanding and his answers. (Luke 2:46–47)

Jesus questions his parents who have been anxiously searching for him:

> Why were you searching for me? Did you not know that I must be in my Father's house? (Luke 2:49)

The scene displays the twelve-year-old Jesus' great knowledge and insight before the priests and teachers. These adult experts have studied and practiced the traditions and law for a long time. The scene also highlights the twelve-year-old Jesus' awareness of his identity and role as son or agent of God his Father. The scene portends Jesus' future roles as both teacher of the divine will as well as agent of divine purposes. It also aligns him with other major male figures who were said as children to display prodigious understanding, such as Moses (Philo, *Moses* 1.21–24), Samuel (Josephus, *Ant.* 5.348), and Josephus, who claims that at age fourteen he had greater knowledge of the law than the chief priests and elite men (*Life* 8–9). We should note that Josephus' claim is made close to the time of the writing of Luke's Gospel.

The long tradition of scenes of childhood actions that foreshadow future greatness includes Alexander the Great. In the absence of his father King Philip, the child Alexander entertains envoys from Macedonia's enemy, the king of Persia. His interaction with these adults is both friendly and perceptive. He impresses the envoys with questions that were neither "childish nor trivial." Instead, Alexander questions them about the roads into Persia and the military "prowess and might" of the king and the Persians (Plutarch, *Alexander* 5).

The significance of his questions is not just to display adult-like conversation and impress the Persians. Unknown to the Persians, Alexander performs a manly role way beyond his physical years in collecting military intelligence that he will draw on in his subsequent military campaign against the Persians. The child Alexander combines charm, strategic insight, military astuteness, and forethought to outwit the Persians.

Plutarch narrates another incident of the Alexander's exceptional abilities as a child (Plutarch, *Alexander* 5). A horse was brought to Alexander's father, King Philip, but it seemed "savage and intractable," unable to be tamed. Philip dismisses it, but Alexander protests, complaining that the adults lack "skill and courage" to manage the horse. Predictably, the child Alexander subdues and rides the horse,

Portents of Greatness

named Bucephalas. Philip is so impressed that he predicts that Alexander will not be able to be contained by Macedonia, thereby anticipating his future role as world conqueror. The scene not only displays Alexander's childhood confidence, courage, and skill. It exhibits his insight and demonstrates his ability to dominate an apparently intractable force, portending his future dominance as a military warrior and conqueror while often riding Bucephalas.

While Plutarch emphasizes the military prowess of Alexander as a child, Suetonius emphasizes another skill that powerful men needed to exercise domination. Being skilled in the art of rhetoric was crucial for powerful men. Parallel to military skill, it was a means of dominating others, persuading allies and subordinates, whether political, legal, or military, to a particular point of view or course of action. In their childhood, future emperors are shown to demonstrate rhetorical skill.

Accordingly, Suetonius (*Deified Augustus* 8.1) describes the twelve-year-old Augustus delivering a funeral oration to a crowd assembled in honor of his grandmother Julia.

The young Tiberius betters Augustus by three years. As a nine-year-old, "he delivered a eulogy of his dead father from the rostra" (Suetonius, *Tiberius* 7). The young Galba, emperor for seven months between June 68 CE and January 69 CE, also displays rhetorical skills as a child in speaking the eulogy at his grandmother Livia's funeral (Suetonius, *Gaius Caligula* 10.1).

Suetonius is more expansive in his praise of the youthful Titus for his "bodily and mental gifts" (*Deified Titus* 3). Suetonius praises Titus' memory, his "aptitude for almost all the arts, both of war and of peace. Skillful in arms and horsemanship, he made speeches and wrote verses in Latin and Greek," as well as demonstrating musical skills. Notable is the inclusion of the standard manly means of domination, namely military and rhetorical skills. Suetonius constructs the youthful Titus so as to anticipate his subsequent power as emperor.

The intertextuality between these accounts that portend imperial greatness and Luke's scene concerning the talented twelve-year-old Jesus performs several functions. One is that it places Jesus among these great men, including Emperors Augustus (Luke 2:1) and Tiberius (Luke 3:1), whom the Gospel mentions. A second function is that the scene sets Jesus in both imitative and contentious relationships with these emperors. In identifying Jesus as "son of God" (1:32; 2:49), Luke's Gospel employs an imperial title (*divi filius*) in promoting Jesus as a similarly sanctioned figure, but one of greater significance as agent of God and not of Rome.[8]

CONCLUSION

We have noted that the accounts of the birth of Jesus in the Gospels of Matthew and Luke include distinctive features: predictions of future greatness; dreams; unusual characters (magi); a mobile star; an endangered child; a wonder-child. As demonstrated, these features are common in narratives of the births and lives of famous men, especially emperors, in the Roman world. Intertextuality between the features of Jesus' birth and dominant Roman men establishes Jesus among the great men, yet redefined as a ruler and agent of *divine*, not Roman, purposes.

---

8. Billings, "At the Age of 12," 88–89.

DISCUSSION QUESTIONS

1. Prophecies, dreams, and portents accompany the births of important men. What role do prophecies of future greatness play in defining powerful Roman males such as Aeneas?

2. How do the Gospels of Matthew and Luke employ this strategy for Jesus?

3. What role do dreams play?

4. What role do portents or omens play in accounts of the births of Emperors Augustus or Vespasian? And Jesus in Matthew's Gospel?

5. What is the role of the motifs of the endangered child and the *wunderkind*?

5

JESUS

Teacher of Societal Structures and Practices

THE GOSPELS BEGIN BY constructing Jesus' genealogies, origins, and phenomena-laden birth, thereby setting Jesus among the great men of his political age and (re)defining his greatness as agent not of the imperial purposes but of divine purposes. Those predictions of future greatness are elaborated in the accounts of Jesus' public activity. In this chapter I consider the intertextuality between the accounts of Jesus as a teacher who outlines a social vision for how to live in God's empire, and traditions involving Greek and Roman founder figures who provide constitutions and teach social practices for their societies.

JESUS: FOUNDER-TEACHER AND SOCIETAL VISIONARY

The Gospels introduce Jesus announcing the presence of God's empire or rule in his teaching:[1]

> From that time Jesus began to proclaim, "Repent, for the empire of the heavens has come near." ... Jesus went throughout Galilee, teaching in their synagogues and proclaiming the good news of the empire.... When Jesus saw the crowds, he went up the mountain; and after he sat down, his disciples came to him. Then he began to speak, and taught them, saying .... (Matt 4:17—5:2, author trans)

Mark's introduction of Jesus' teaching mission is comparable:

> Now after John was arrested, Jesus came to Galilee, proclaiming the good news of God, and saying, "The time is fulfilled, and the empire of God has come near; repent, and believe in the good news." (Mark 1:14–15, author trans)

In Luke's Gospel, in a synagogue in Nazareth, Luke's Jesus reads from Isa 58 and 61 to name examples of his societally transformative activities before summarizing his general mission to manifest the empire or reign of God:

> The Spirit of the Lord is upon me, because he has anointed me to bring good news to the poor. He has sent me to proclaim release to the

---

1. The translation "empire" represents the Greek term often translated "kingdom," "reign," "rule," or "kingdom." My translation highlights the imperial framework in which the divine action and Jesus' commission are framed. Such framing poses for interpreters the challenge of reframing and relanguaging expressions of divine action in the world.

> captives and recovery of sight to the blind, to let the oppressed go free, to proclaim the year of the Lord's favor.... I must proclaim the good news of the empire of God to the other cities also; for I was sent for this purpose. (Luke 4:18–19, 43; author trans)

John's Gospel introduces Jesus as the bringer of life and God's empire:

> What has come into being in him was life.... Very truly, I tell you, no one can see the empire of God without being born from above. (John 1:3–4; 3:3 author trans)

Having constructed Jesus' public activity from the outset as announcing God's empire, the Gospels proceed to elaborate Jesus teaching about the practices and structures of life in the empire of God. In doing so, he joins a long line of great men who shaped society with their teaching and law-making.[2] I discuss three "ancient" examples (Lycurgus; Solon; Moses) before moving to two first-century imperial examples, Augustus and Nero, and the social vision of Jesus.

LYCURGUS OF SPARTA

According to Plutarch, the legendary eighth-century BCE Spartan Lycurgus visited Delphi to consult the oracle. The Pythian priestess greeted him as "beloved of the gods, and rather god than man," and assured him that the god "had granted his prayer for good laws" (Plutarch, *Lycurgus*, 5, also 29). He returns to Sparta to "revolutionize the civil polity" of a diseased society (*Lycurgus* 5).

His polity is committed to societal equality, military fitness that begins with the upbringing of children, and

2. Szegedy-Maszak, "Legends."

austerity. In a context of "dreadful inequality" and in order "to banish insolence and envy and crime and luxury, and poverty and wealth," and to establish "uniformity and equality," he orders land to be redistributed, and property to be divided (Plutarch, *Lycurgus* 8–9). His austerity program banished arts, attacked luxury and social hierarchy, instituted common meals and food, and forbade luxury and extravagance in housing and furnishings (*Lycurgus* 9–10, 13). He regulated the behavior and clothing of women, encouraged marriage, and regulated its conduct marked by "self-restraint and moderation" (*Lycurgus* 14–15). Particularly, he ordered procreation and the regimented raising of children akin to that of training animals (16–21).

As Lavery emphasizes, such training and education were basic to Lycurgus' social vision and control.[3] Plutarch (*Lycurgus* 30.4) comments,

> For a good leader makes good followers, and just as the final attainment of the art of horsemanship is to make a horse gentle and tractable, so it is the task of the science of government to implant obedience in men (sic!).

This implanting of obedience meant that Lycurgus did not commit any laws to writing since he thought that if they were "implanted in the habits and training of its citizens . . . by education," they would be more secure than if obedience to written laws was compelled (Plutarch, *Lycurgus* 13).

> He trained his fellow-citizens to have neither the wish nor the ability to live for themselves; but like bees they were to make themselves always integral parts of the whole community, clustering together about their leader. (*Lycurgus* 25.3)

---

3. Lavery, "Training," 370–72.

It can be noted that animal images to depict the training and compliance of citizens with Lycurgus' societal vision pervade Plutarch's presentation of Lycurgus' approach to social order.

SOLON OF ATHENS C. 600 BCE

According to Plutarch, some understood that Solon received an oracle at Delphi that authorized him to address the conflicted socio-political situation in Athens marked by division and disputes over forms of government and disparities between the rich and the poor indebted to the rich (Plutarch, *Solon* 13.1–2; 14.4). Solon sought to de-escalate tensions in societal interactions by checking the injustice and rapacity of the citizens with written laws (*Solon* 5.2). One part of his program was to cancel debts and repeal most of Draco's harsh laws and death penalties (*Solon* 15–24).

Solon's goal was not social equality, so he maintained elite power by dividing the population hierarchically into four groups based on wealth (land, possessions, and production). He prohibited the lowest level from holding public office. Yet he made concessions to them in setting up two councils (powerful leaders; common people) and giving all citizens the right to bring action against a wrongdoer. Solon's program met with acceptance by some and rejection by others so that divisions between rich and poor and over differing forms of government continued (Plutarch, *Solon* 25, 29).

MOSES

Traditions about Moses as the one who transmitted to Israel the social vision he received on Mount Sinai from the deity have spanned the Hebrew Bible, its Greek translation,

Jesus

known as the Septuagint, and first-century writers such as Philo of Alexandria and Josephus of Rome. Josephus claims Moses to be the most ancient shaper of society or legislator in the world (Josephus, *Against Apion* 2.154).[4] He did not advocate monarchy, oligarchy, or mass rule as others had done; instead his social vision was a theocracy that combined weekly instruction in the will of God with practical training (2.164, 173–75). Josephus elaborates Moses' social vision as encompassing the worship of God (2.190–98), various social structures such as marriage, education, honoring parents, inclusion of outsiders, supplying the daily material needs of all (2.199–214), penalties and rewards (2.215–19). He regards this divinely-authorized social structure and practice as superior to any Greek vision and practice (2.220–96).

AUGUSTUS

Augustus shaped the structures and practices of the Roman Empire in the first century, not by his teaching and formulation of a state constitution, as with Lycurgus and Solon, but by decrees and actions. Augustus emerged from the violent decade of retaliations, civil strife, and power struggles that followed Julius Caesar's assassination in 44 BCE as the victor after defeating Antony in the battle of Actium in 31 BCE. The decade had taken a societal toll in terms of widespread weariness of war, declining faith in the gods, and collapsing ancestral values.

With a range of strategies, Augustus set about a political, moral, and religious renewal of the empire. Celebrations

4. Josephus employs here a pattern of community definition comprising origin, governance, and practice. Dionysius of Halicarnassus (*Roman Antiquities* 1.9—2.29) employs the same pattern for Rome. See Carter, *Matthew and the Margins*, 11–14 for analysis of Matthew's Gospel in these terms.

of his victory constructed him as the bringer of peace and unity and chosen by the gods. He consolidated control of the armies that had previously been loyal to his rivals, maintained a disciplined standing army,[5] and settled veterans with land and financial grants. He exercised political control in Rome and across the empire through visits, alliances, appointed legates, and colonies. He sought to restore traditional values of marriage and family, as well as piety toward the gods to ensure their continued blessing on the empire.

By the year 17 BCE, there was growing optimism. Celebrations proclaimed a new age or *Saeculum*, a golden age. Horace wrote a hymn addressed to Apollo and Diana, a hymn of the ages (*Carmen saeculare*) performed as part of the celebratory games by twenty-seven young women and men, symbols of the empire's piety and future fecundity.[6] The hymn encapsulates Augustus' social vision. It seeks many births, renewed marriage morals, peace, and the abundant fertility of the earth in producing fruits, cattle, and grain. It locates Augustus' reign in relation to the myth of Aeneas as the founder of Rome chosen by the gods. It celebrates and thereby affirms the reversal of and improvement in social conditions and interactions under Augustus' rule in declaring that "trust and peace and honor and ancient manners venture back among us and long neglected upright conduct; plenty comes too." It seeks the gods to prosper Roman power through the ages. The hymn affirms Augustus' accomplishments and anticipates a god-blessed future of social morals, children, abundance, and Roman dominance under his rule.

Toward the end of his life, Augustus wrote his *Res Gestae* (hereafter *RG*), an account of his accomplishments that,

5. Suetonius, *Deified Augustus* 24.
6. Zanker, *Power of Images*, 169–72.

whatever its purpose,[7] identifies key aspects of his societal vision.[8]

As the opening lines indicate, fundamental to that vision is Roman military domination in making "the entire world subject to the power of the Roman people." Augustus avenged those who killed Julius Caesar and defeated them in war (*RG* 2) as well as waging "many wars on land and on sea . . . throughout the whole world," destroying enemies, but also displaying clemency or mercy to peoples who sought forgiveness (*RG* 3). This military dominance included victories in Spain and Gaul, which "secured peace on land and sea throughout the whole empire of the Roman people" (*RG* 12–13, 26). To honor the accomplishment, the Senate commissioned an altar (*Ara Pacis*) in Rome dedicated in 9 BCE to *Pax*, the Roman goddess of Peace. Augustus defeated pirates, captured thirty thousand rebels, received oaths of allegiance from "the provinces of Gaul, Spain, Africa, Sicily, and Sardinia," expanded the empire's territory including the addition of Egypt, received submission from numerous rulers, and exercised generous gifts of land and money to veterans settled in various colonies on conquered and confiscated land (*RG* 2, 16, 25–33). He restored power to the Senate even as he reformed its operations and expanded administrative positions and appointments, which undergirded his power (*RG* 34; Suetonius, *Deified Augustus* 35–37).

Augustus secured this military and political domination with acts of piety. He dedicated numerous temples and restored "eighty-two temples of the gods in the city," including temples to Jupiter and Mars Ultor (the Avenger; *RG* 19–21). The political-theological reasoning follows a circular sequence that begins with piety in honoring the

7. Harrison, "Augustan Rome," 5.
8. Translation in Eck, *Augustus*, 134–47.

gods with sacrifices, prayers, priesthoods, and temples to secure divine favor. Such honoring was understood to gain divine blessings that ensured Roman troops were successful in war. Victory resulted and peace was established, comprising domination, safety, security, abundance, and fertility (at least for some). The same sequence is evident in the side panels and carvings of the Ara Pacis.[9]

Accompanying these acts of piety was an emphasis on reforming morals and public virtue. Augustus declares he became "the guardian of laws and morals with supreme powers" (*RG* 6). He claims to have revived "many exemplary practices of our ancestors . . . and transmitted to posterity many models of conduct to be imitated" (*RG* 8). According to Suetonius (*Deified Augustus* 34), Augustus enacted laws "on extravagance, on adultery and chastity, on bribery, and on the encouragement of marriage."

In addition, Augustus secured public favor in Rome with numerous acts of patronage and benevolence. He provided grain for the city (*RG* 5, 18), set up a system of night watchmen to protect against fire, took actions to protect the city from flooding from the Tiber, acted against those causing civic instability, and administered justice in a conscientious and lenient manner (Suetonius, *Deified Augustus* 30, 32–33). He made cash grants to inhabitants and soldiers (*RG* 15), secured the water supply, and provided numerous entertainments (Suetonius, *Deified Augustus* 42–45; *RG* 20, 22–23). He undertook much rebuilding of Rome itself (*RG* 20; *Deified Augustus* 29) so that it should be "adorned as the dignity of the empire demanded, . . . he found it built of brick and left it in marble" (Suetonius, *Deified Augustus* 23–24, 29).

Augustus ends his *Res Gestae* by narrating that the Senate and Roman people gave him an inscribed shield that

9. Crossan, "Roman Imperial Theology."

Jesus

recognized his "virtue, clemency, justice, and piety" (*RG* 34).[10] The four characteristics summarized not just Augustus' personal qualities but his social vision for the empire, at least as understood by elites. He also accepted the designation, "Father of the Fatherland," (*pater patriae*), a title that envisioned the empire as a great household ruled over by a benign father.[11] Many poor inhabitants of the empire, however, did not experience his imperial vision, structures, and practices to be benign.

NERO: SENECA'S SOCIAL VISION OF MERCY

In 54 CE, when Claudius died, the seventeen-year-old Nero became emperor. "He declared that he would rule according to the principles of Augustus and he let slip no opportunity for acts of generosity and mercy" (Suetonius, *Nero* 10.1). In his treatise *De Clementia*, written in c. 55 CE, the philosopher and imperial adviser Seneca instructs Nero on being a merciful or clement, rather than cruel, ruler. Seneca elaborates that mercy is not just a personal virtue but a way of shaping a compliant and appreciative society.[12]

Seneca addresses Nero directly and begins by recognizing in a monologue his immense power as "arbiter of life and death for the nations; it rests in my power what each man's lot and state shall be" (*De Clementia* 1.1–2; hereafter *De Clem*). The key issue concerns how Nero will use his

---

10. Elliott, *Arrogance of Nations*.

11. Carter, "God as 'Father,'" 83–91. The image constructs the emperor as savior and benefactor of life, ruler of the world, judge and lawgiver, creator and shaper of a people, sender of agents, recipient of honors.

12. Dowling, *Clemency*, 194–203. Compare Pliny's *Panegyricus* in which Pliny affirms Trajan's social practice and provides an example for successors.

massive power to shape society; who will benefit? (*De Clem* 1.3.3).

Dowling argues that Seneca's efforts to shape Nero's behavior are fundamentally pragmatic.[13] An emperor who behaves with clemency and displays merciful actions towards his subjects secures their love. Subjects love a merciful ruler who, though their superior, is a friend who is concerned for their safety and wellbeing. A cruel ruler is a monster from whom subjects flee. But for a merciful ruler, subjects out of devotion and loyalty will readily give their lives to protect their ruler (*De Clem* 1.3.2–4).

A merciful ruler benefits the whole state. Using the image of the body, Seneca argues that the ruler is the great and rational mind that orders the state, unites it, and provides the breath of life that elevates all its inhabitants so that they are not a burden to themselves or prey for others (*De Clem* 1.3.5–4.1). The force of Seneca's argument emerges in his claim that the very existence of the empire depends on such an emperor. His absence "would be the destruction of the Roman peace, such a calamity will force the fortune of a mighty people to its downfall" (*De Clem* 1.4.2–3). A ruler lacking mercy results in wars and actions expressive of "cruel and inexorable anger" (*De Clem* 1.5.3, 6).

Mercy involves hierarchy since only the superior or more powerful ruler can grant life to an inferior and this display of mercy reflects positively on the superior rank and status of the ruler (*De Clem* 1.5.6–7). Yet the enactment of mercy involves reciprocity. Since all do wrong, all need it, including a ruler (*De Clem* 1.6.2–4). The emperor is to treat people with mercy just as he hopes to acquire merciful beneficence from the gods (*De Clem* 1.7.1). The gods are to be the ruler's model: "he should wish so to be to his subjects, as he would wish the gods to be to himself" (*De Clem* 1.7.2).

13. Dowling, *Clemency*, 196.

Jesus

The pay-off in displaying mercy is that it breeds and encourages obedience and loyalty among subjects (*De Clem* 24.2).

By contrast, a cruel ruler or angry tyrant causes many to cower in terror (*De Clem* 1.8.5). Repeated punishment crushes the hatred of a few but results in the hatred of all; killing opponents multiplies enemies (1.8.7). A cruel ruler rules through fear (1.12.4). While merciful rulers are honored, they are also safe from life-ending attacks from opponents whereas tyrants are vulnerable and short-lived (1.11.4). Cruel rulers or tyrants find pleasure in punishment, enjoy observing pain and suffering, and seek to inflict more of it (*De Clem* 1.25).

Mercy requires restraint in relation to punishment of wrongdoers or treatment of opponents. Augustus provides an example of restraint in punishment and of turning enemies to friends (*De Clem* 1.9–10).

> Mercy means restraining the mind from vengeance when it has the power to take it, or the leniency of a superior towards an inferior in fixing punishment. . . . (M)ercy is the moderation which remits something from the punishment that is deserved and due. . . . Mercy consists in stopping short of what might have been deservedly imposed. (*De Clem* 2.3.1–2)

Seneca envisions Nero ruling a society in which he uses his immense power not to harm subjects but to benefit them. Imitating merciful gods means, for example, exercising leniency and moderating punishment. Dowling notes, though, that Seneca's social vision "had little lasting effect on the emperor's behavior."[14] He chose cruelty over clemency.

---

14. Dowling, *Clemency*, 209.

THE GOSPELS

These discussions of Lycurgus, Solon, Moses, Augustus, and Nero (addressed by Seneca) provide examples from a long tradition of key figures who have provided social visions, structures, and practices for their societies. The Gospels locate Jesus in this tradition by constructing him as the teacher of the vision, structures, and practices that constitute life in the empire of God. This section explores the intertextuality between this tradition of key figures and the Gospels' presentations of Jesus. Because of space restrictions I will mostly concentrate on Matthew's Gospel and its considerable concentration of teaching material.

The Matthean construction of the beginning of Jesus' public activity follows Mark's Gospel (Matt 4:17; Mark 1:15). In both accounts, Jesus announces that God's empire "has come near." The image of God's empire evokes Hebrew Bible traditions concerning God as the king who rules over and orders creation and the nations (Exod 15:11–13; Pss 95–100). Some nations resist this reign, so the traditions recognize that while God reigns, God's rule is not yet established fully. In the future, though, God will establish God's rule fully over all nations (Mic 2:12–13; Dan 7:11–14; Zeph 3:14–20).

The Gospels construct Jesus as the agent of these purposes. The verb translated "has come near" holds together dimensions of arrival and nearness, presence and future. Jesus discloses both present and future dimensions of God's purposes.

Moreover, he does so in a politically charged context. The Greek term that the Gospels use to refer to the "empire of God" names various empires: Babylon, Media, Persia, Macedonia, the Seleucids, and the contemporary Roman

Empire.[15] Jesus' announcement of God's empire and teaching about its structures and practices occurs in this context. The Gospel narratives heighten this conflictual context by setting the story of Jesus in Galilee and Judea. These areas were colonized by Roman power, represented by a Roman governor, troops, taxes, and local leaders (priests, Pharisees, Sadducees, scribes, elders) who were allied with but submissive to Roman control and interests.

What relationship exists, then, between God's empire and Rome's empire? The interactions are complex and multivalent. They range across coexistence and accommodation, opposition and conflict, imitation and mimicry. One example of imitation is the fact that the divine purposes are languaged with the term "empire." The things of Caesar are attributed to God who will "out-caesar" Caesar to become the supreme ruler of the world.

What does it look like when Jesus announces God's empire to be at work in the midst of Rome's empire? Both Matthew and Mark immediately follow this opening announcement with Jesus calling his first followers, disrupting their daily lives as fishermen and familial relationships, summoning them to a new loyalty and identity, commissioning them to a new mission, and founding a new community (Matt 4:18–22; Mark 1:16–20). Both Gospels follow up with summaries of Jesus' teaching activity and miraculous actions (discussed in the next chapter) that exhibit God's empire at work.

In Luke's Gospel, Jesus elaborates God's empire by citing from Isa 58 and 61. These verses emphasize the transformative nature of God's empire at work in bringing good news to the poor, release to the captives, sight to the blind, freedom to the oppressed, and the year of the Lord's favor.

---

15. Dan 2:37–45; 1 Macc 1:16, 41, 51; Josephus, *J.W.* 1.40; 5.409; 7.40.

These proclamations and actions repair the damage that Rome's empire causes.

In addition to shorter scenes, Matthew's Gospel feature five concentrated blocks of Jesus' teachings about living in God's empire: the Sermon on the Mount (chs 5–7); instructions for mission (ch 10); parables about God's empire (ch 13); instructions for communities of disciples (ch 18), and teaching about the triumphant establishment of God's empire (chs 24–25).[16]

The Sermon on the Mount (Matt 5–7)

The Sermon on the Mount, comprising some 109 verses of teaching attributed to Jesus, elaborates the identity and practices of his followers committed to God's empire.[17] The sermon refers to God's empire seven times, thereby positioning it as the teaching's central focus (5:3, 10, 19–20; 6:10, 33; 7:21).

The opening section articulates nine blessings encountered in oppressive situations where God's favor is experienced along with human actions that share in and manifest the divine purposes (5:3–12). God's favor reverses and transforms imperial injustices encountered by the (literal) powerless poor (the "meek") who seek God's justice. (5:3–6). It provokes actions of mercy, integrity of action and worship, peacemaking, nonviolent dissent from resistant Roman rule (5:7–12). Language such as "peace" and "justice" commonly denote imperial claims; the Gospel contestively redefines the words in terms of divine purposes.[18]

---

16. Compare John 13–17.

17. Luke's Gospel (6:20–49) includes a shorter Sermon on the Plain.

18. Carter, *Matthew and the Margins*, 128–39.

Six further examples of actions of the "exceeding justice/righteousness" that God's empire shapes follow in 5:21–48: community reconciliation, curbing male lust, restricting male power in divorce, trustworthy speech, active nonviolent resistance to evil, and indiscriminate love for neighbors and enemies. Three further acts of justice are named in 6:1–18: acts of mercy, prayer, and fasting regarded in Isa 58 as participating in the struggle against societal injustices. Rejecting cultural practices of public displays of beneficence as a means for elites to gain public honor, status, and power, Jesus' teaching emphasizes *God* as the audience for acts of justice. The Lord's Prayer (6:9–13) prays for justice in petitions for God's empire to come, God's will to be done on earth as in heaven, the supply of daily bread, and forgiveness of debt.[19]

The emphasis on justice continues in 6:19–34 in a rejection of the pursuit of material possessions, a recognition that such a pursuit is incompatible with serving God, and an exhortation to seek God's empire in the provision of daily necessities. The following verses identify further practices of compassionate correction of other followers, persistent prayer, and indiscriminate love in action (Matt 7:1–12).

The sermon ends with an emphasis on future eschatological accountability to God for living faithfully to Jesus' teaching (7:13–27). This accountability comprises reward as incentive for obedience. It employs the common "two ways" metaphor to emphasize the counter-cultural way of life that followers choose to pursue while rejecting dominant cultural practices (7:13–14). Verses 15–23 raise alerts about false prophets and their way of life, which will lead to their condemnation. Verses 24–27 employ a binary

---

19. Compare Luke 11:2–4 for a shorter version. Carter, *Matthew and the Margins*, 140–70.

structure to contrast doing or not doing God's will as taught by Jesus and the eschatological consequences of vindication or condemnation.

Matthew's remaining teaching chapters

Chapter 10 addresses the interaction between the community of followers and the larger imperial society. Jesus followers are defined as a mission community. Imitation and redefinition vis-à-vis Rome are evident. Rome's mission comprises establishing an "empire without end and to be lords of the world who crown peace with justice, spare the vanquished and crush the proud" (Virgil, *Aeneid* 1.254–82; 6.851–83). Jesus' followers are commissioned to continue Jesus' mission of announcing God's empire, and of performing his transformative actions that repair the damage done to casualties of Roman power (10:7–8).

Chapter 13 comprises seven parables about God's empire. The parables explain why some people discern Jesus to be the agent of God's empire while others, especially the Rome-sanctioned local leaders, do not. The parable of the sower or the soils, for example, recognizes the work of the devil, the experience of trouble, the cares of the world, and the lure of wealth as factors that prevent discerning God's empire (13:18–23). Other parables identify other challenges: God's empire exists in the midst of and coexists with the structures of the everyday imperial world (13:24–30). Its presence is very small and apparently inconsequential in the present compared to its future grand and glorious establishment (13:31–32, 33). But it is worth giving everything to discern the presence of God's empire (13:44–45). And followers can be assured that in the end God's empire will be established in all its victorious fullness (13:36–43, 47–50).

The fourth teaching block focuses on community relationships among Jesus-followers (ch 18). Jesus' teaching has established that following him on the way of the cross is challenging. It cannot be done in isolation; it is a communal way of life. It comprises, and is sustained by, a network of communal practices and interdependent relationships that Jesus identifies in this chapter. Humility (not imperial greatness and domination), vulnerability and powerlessness, sustaining rather than despising one another, resolving conflicts in a communal process, and the practice of forgiveness constitute communal practices.

The final teaching block turns to the final establishment and victory of God's empire (chs 24–25). Jesus elaborates signs of his return and of the end of the age. He offers, for example, a scenario of a final battle in which he returns to destroy Roman power (24:27–31). And he anticipates the final accountability of the nations in which they are judged according to how they have treated the casualties of Rome's empire, the vulnerable and powerless with whom Jesus identifies (25:31–46). Have they fed the hungry, given drink to the thirsty, welcomed the stranger, clothed the homeless, cared for the sick, visited the imprisoned? This glimpse of the final judgment provides a divine mandate for repairing the damage inflicted by Rome's elite-benefitting imperial world.

These five major collections of Jesus' teaching in Matthew set out structures and practices that are shaped by and manifest God's empire. Other parts of Matthew's Gospel, whether shorter sections or different genres, perform similar functions. For example, short conflictual scenes emphasize mercy and love as markers of the daily life and practices of Jesus' followers (9:13; 12:7; 22:37–39). Chapters 19–20 comprise a series of scenes structured on the basis of the topics and power relationships in ideal elite households:

husband rules over wife, father over children, master over slaves, and the head male provides for the household in society. Chapters 19–20 employ this structure but revise and critique it in re-envisioning household structures. Part of the instruction is a rejection of the domination and tyrannical ways of imperial "great men" and gentile rulers. Instead, followers of Jesus are to seek the wellbeing of others (20:24–27).

CONCLUSION

This chapter has examined the intertextuality between Jesus as a teacher of a societal vision, practices, and structures, and men who as ruling leaders set forth their societal visions, practices, and structures in various formats. The intertextuality continues to set Jesus among the great men, and clearly constructs him not as a spiritualized figure but as the exponent of societal practices expressive of the empire of God that both imitate and contest imperial ways.

DISCUSSION QUESTIONS

1. Describe the societal vision put forward by Lycurgus or Solon or Moses.

2. What is Augustus' societal vision for the Roman Empire?

3. What sort of societal vision does the philosopher Seneca offer the young Emperor Nero?

4. What sort of societal vision does Jesus offer in Matthew's Gospel? How does it interact with Roman imperial visions, structures, and practices?

6

MIRACLES, SIGNS, AND WONDERS

GOSPELS, GODS, AND HUMAN HEROES

THE SYNOPTIC GOSPELS OF Matthew, Mark, and Luke present Jesus' public activity as marked by the performance of miraculous works: healing the sick, exorcising the demon-possessed, raising the dead, controlling nature, and manipulating inanimate materials like bread, and fish. Though not as prolific, and using the language of signs, John's Gospel similarly presents Jesus as controlling inanimate materials: turning water into wine (John 2:1–11), multiplying bread and fish (6:1–15), walking on water (6:16–21), healing the sick (the official's son, John 4:46–54; the paralyzed man, 5:1–9; the man born blind, 9:1–41), and raising the dead (Lazarus, John 11:1–44; Jesus' own resurrection, 11:25?).

Miraculous actions attributed to both gods and human heroes are widely attested in the ancient world.[1] For example, various gods are identified as sources of healings, such as Israel's God (Ps 103:3), Asclepius, and the goddess Isis.[2] Human healers include Moses (Num 21:4–9), Elisha (2 Kgs 5:1–27), Honi the circle-dweller and Hanina ben Dosa,[3] Pythagoras, and Apollonius of Tyana.[4] Hercules and Asclepius are gods who raise people from the dead,[5] as do the humans Elijah (1 Kgs 17:17–24), Elisha (2 Kgs 4:18–37), Apollonius, and Asclepiades.[6] Gods—such as Poseidon, Isis and Serapis, and Israel's God[7]—and humans, such as Pythagoras and Apollonius,[8] as well as Moses (Exod 14:15–29), Joshua (Josh 3:1–17), Elijah (1 Kgs 17:1; 18:45), and Elisha (2 Kgs 2:6–15) exhibited power over the natural world, such as calming storms, dividing seas, and walking on water. Other gods, such as Dionysus, are said to manipulate natural elements, turning water into wine, while human heroes, such as Moses (Exod 16:1–18), Elijah (1 Kgs 17:8–16), and Elisha (2 Kgs 4:42–44) manipulate resources to create abundant food.[9] Apollonius and Tobit

---

1. Cotter, *Miracles: Sourcebook*; Cotter, "Miracle Stories."

2. For texts, Asclepius, Edelstein, *Asclepius*; Cotter, *Miracles: Sourcebook*, 15–30, 30–34 (Isis); Cotter, "Miracle Stories," 170–72.

3. Avery-Peck, "Galilean Charismatic Piety"; Vermes, *Jesus*, 69–82.

4. Cotter, *Miracles: Sourcebook* 37–38, 43–45; "Miracle Stories," 172–75.

5. Cotter, *Miracles: Sourcebook*, Hercules, 13–14; Asclepius 26, 29–30.

6. Cotter, *Miracles: Sourcebook*, 45–47.

7. Cotter, *Miracles: Sourcebook*, 133, 149 (Poseidon), 135–37 (Isis and Serapis), 138–42, 149–50 (Israel's God).

8. Cotter, *Miracles: Sourcebook*, 143–46, 151–52.

9. Cotter, *Miracles: Sourcebook*, 164–68.

Miracles, Signs, and Wonders

(Tobit 6:1–18; 7:15—8:9) exorcize demons.[10] The ancient world was well familiar with miracles, signs, and wonders.

In this chapter, I explore the intertextuality between the Gospel accounts of Jesus' miracles and one subset of the heroes named above, namely miracles performed by ruling figures, particularly Roman emperors. Accounts of miracle-working rulers existed long before the writing of the Gospels toward the end of the first century CE. Significantly, accounts of wonder-working emperors gain some prominence around the same time as the writing of the Gospels late in the first century. I will suggest that while these imperial traditions function to display and augment the ruler/emperor's divinely sanctioned power, the intertextuality with the Gospel stories indicates that accounts of Jesus miracle-working function in a context of imperial domination in both imitative and contestive ways. I argue that the Gospels imitate the imperial interest in augmenting Jesus by constructing him as a divinely sanctioned agent, though not of the empire of Rome but of the empire of God. Yet while the imperial accounts uphold imperial practices and structures, the Gospel accounts destabilize and repair the normativity of somatic damage inflicted by Rome's empire. The Gospels employ a different reality constituted by the empire of God that both contests, and in places imitates, Rome's empire.[11]

---

10. Cotter, *Miracles: Sourcebook*, 83–89.

11. This argument bears some semblance to that of Betcher. "Disability," though I recognize more ambiguity, notably the presence of imitation of imperial ways, than is present in her argument.

RULERS AND MIRACLES BEFORE THE EMPEROR VESPASIAN (69 CE–79 CE)

A long tradition associates rulers with various miracles. King David exorcizes Saul (Josephus, *Ant.* 6.166–69). King Solomon has power over demons, which he transmits to others:[12]

> And God granted him knowledge of the art used against demons for the benefit and healing of men (sic). He also composed incantations by which illnesses are relieved, and left behind forms of exorcisms with which those possessed by demons drive them out. (Josephus, *Ant.* 8.43)

The Persian King Xerxes (d. 465 BCE) was understood to have performed a god-like act in "walking dryshod on water." Actually, he led his army over the sea at the Hellespont by means of a bridge made out of boats linked together, an act that people understood to make him equal to the god Poseidon:

> of all men under the sun that man is most powerful and in might no whit inferior to the gods themselves who is able to accomplish the seemingly impossible—if it should be his will, to have men walk dryshod over the sea. . . . [H]e led his infantry through the sea, riding upon a chariot just like Poseidon in Homer's description . . . . (Dio Chrysostom, *Third Discourse on Kingship*, 30–31)

Alexander "the Great" is said to go one further. The Jewish writer Josephus defends the accuracy of his account of Moses' exploit of parting the sea in the exodus of

---

12. Duling, "Solomon."

Israelites from Egypt by comparing it to Alexander's accomplishment of parting the Pamphylian sea:

> the hosts of Alexander king of Macedon, men born but the other day, beheld the Pamphylian Sea retire before them and, when another road there was none, offer a passage through itself, what time it pleased God to overthrow the Persian empire; and on that all are agreed who have recorded Alexander's exploits. (Josephus, *Ant.* 2.347–48)

King Pyrrhus of Epirus (d. 272 BCE), an area of Greece on the western Balkans, and a militant opponent of Rome, was associated with healing. The spleen was his speciality, which he healed by applying pressure from his right foot (especially his big toe!). And he extended his healing to the most poor (Plutarch, *Pyrrhus* 3.4–5).

An interesting story constructs Julius Caesar trying to display his vast authority by subduing the sea.

> At night, accordingly, after disguising himself in the dress of a slave, he went on board, threw himself down as one of no account, and kept quiet. [But stormy weather endangers the boat and the captain orders the sailors to return to their point of departure.] But Caesar, perceiving this, disclosed himself, took the master of the boat by the hand, who was terrified at sight of him, and said: "Come, good man, be bold and fear naught; thou carryest Caesar and Caesar's fortune in thy boat." The sailors forgot the storm, and laying to their oars, tried with all alacrity to force their way down the river. But since it was impossible, after taking much water and running great hazard at the mouth of the river, Caesar very reluctantly suffered the captain to

put about. (Plutarch, *Caesar* 38:2-6; also Dio Cassius, 46.1-4).

In a much shorter version of the story, Suetonius (*Deified Julius* 58.2) emphasizes Caesar's courage and determination in countering the boat captain's initial decision to turn back. But Suetonius does not narrate Caesar's subsequent failure to calm the sea! The upside of the scene is that Caesar survives and is not drowned by the tempestuous sea.

The Alexandrian Jewish writer Philo recognizes that the Emperor Augustus miraculously accomplished peace in the empire when he defeated Antony at the battle of Actium in 31 BCE. Philo uses two images to describe Augustus' imperial domination. Philo says that Augustus "calmed the torrential storms on every side," and he "healed the pestilences" or the diseases that afflicted the world. The first image reflects control over the natural order; the second image reflects control over diseases that afflict the human condition:

> the whole human race exhausted by mutual slaughter was on the verge of utter destruction, had it not been for one man and leader Augustus whom men fitly call the averter of evil. This is the Caesar who calmed the torrential storms on every side, who healed the pestilences common to Greeks and barbarians, pestilences which descending from the south and the east[,] coursed to the west and north[,] sowing the seeds of calamity over the places and waters which lay between. (Philo, *Embassy to Gaius* 144-45)

Philo's use of these two images is metaphorical. Yet his description attests an association in the first century CE of emperors with miracles. Specifically, Philo associates the Emperor Augustus with the calming of storms and the healing of diseases.

Miracles, Signs, and Wonders

Some five hundred or so years after the Persian King Xerxes used boats to cross the sea at the Hellespont, the Emperor Gaius Caligula (d. 41 CE) emulates but exceeds this godlike accomplishment. He also uses a fleet of ships, but spans a much greater distance (Suetonius, *Gaius Caligula* 19). Josephus introduces the episode by commenting that Caligula sought in this act to demonstrate his lordship over land and sea:

> He considered it his privilege as lord of the sea to require the same service from the sea as he received from the land. (Josephus, *Ant.* 19.1, 5–6)

These instances attest a long tradition spanning various cultures that associated rulers with miracles.

MIRACLES INVOLVING EMPEROR VESPASIAN

Three sources attest the Emperor Vespasian's wonder-working activity in Egypt at the beginning of his reign in November 69 CE. Suetonius (*Deified Vespasian* 7.1) explains these miracles in relation to Vespasian's uncertainty concerning his imperial identity, status, and future. He presents the miracles as signs that confirm divine sanction for Vespasian's rule as emperor.[13]

The first sign places the newly minted emperor in Egypt to take possession of it and its grain as vital for Rome's food supply. Suetonius declares that Vespasian "entered the temple of Serapis alone, to consult the auspices as to the duration of his power." During appropriate rituals, Vespasian's freedman, named Basilides, seems to appear mysteriously and to be present with Vespasian. The significance of the vision is that the name "Basilides" evokes the Greek name for king or emperor, and so the vision is

13. Leppin, "Imperial Miracles."

regarded as a confirming sign for Vespasian's imperial identity as supreme ruler or emperor of the Roman Empire. After the rituals, Suetonius says, "immediately letters came with the news that Vitellius had been routed at Cremona and the emperor himself slain at Rome." Vespasian's rival and the ruling imperial claimant Vitellius has been defeated and killed. The god Serapis is presented as providing divine sanction for Vespasian's rule.

Suetonius introduces the second sign by declaring "Vespasian as yet lacked prestige and a certain divinity, so to speak, since he was an unexpected and still new-made emperor." The Latin term translated "prestige" (*auctoritas*) evokes the authoritative status and influence that a powerful person exercises. The term translated "divinity" (*maiestas*) suggests a person's greatness and dignity. The newly acclaimed emperor lacks these identity markers.

Suetonius narrates two healing miracles—restoring sight to a blind person and mobility to a lame person—that augment Vespasian's imperial prestige, authority, and dignity.

> A man of the people who was blind, and another who was lame, came to him together as he sat on the tribunal, begging for the help for their disorders which Serapis had promised in a dream; for the god declared that Vespasian would restore the eyes, if he would spit upon them, and give strength to the leg, if he would deign to touch it with his heel. Though he had hardly any faith that this could possibly succeed, and therefore shrank even from making the attempt, he was at last prevailed upon by his friends and tried both things in public before a large crowd; and with success. (Suetonius, *Deified Vespasian* 7.2)

Miracles, Signs, and Wonders

According to Suetonius, Vespasian struggles to believe Serapis' dream-revealed promise of healing for the disabled men and the commission to Vespasian to be a healer. Nevertheless, not only does Vespasian proceed to heal the two men, he does so with the encouragement of friends "in public before a large crowd." Many witness his success, providing an extensive informal communication network to attest Vespasian's imperial prestige, authority, and dignity as the chosen one of the god Serapis.[14]

Tacitus (*Hist* 4.81–82) offers somewhat different details. He declares Vespasian performed "many miracles," though he narrates only a couple. One involves the healing of the blind man. Tacitus replaces the lame man with a man who has a "useless" hand. Tacitus frames the scenes, though, with a similar emphasis on expressions of divine favor for Vespasian.

Tacitus narrates that while Vespasian waits at Alexandria to sail to Rome:

> many marvels occurred to mark the favour of heaven and a certain partiality of the gods toward him. One of the common people of Alexandria, well known for his loss of sight, threw himself before Vespasian's knees, praying him with groans to cure his blindness, being so directed by the god Serapis . . . and he besought the emperor to deign to moisten his cheeks and eyes with his spittle. Another, whose hand was useless, prompted by the same god, begged Caesar to step and trample on it.

Tacitus continues by saying that Vespasian initially ridicules these requests, but the petitioners persisted in their appeals. Vespasian sways between the fear of ridicule

---

14. Suetonius adds a third sign, the discovery of some antique vases bearing "an image very like Vespasian."

from failure and glory from success. He seeks the views of physicians as to whether these ailments might be healed by human interventions. Vespasian becomes convinced that it

> was the wish of the gods, and it might be that the emperor had been chosen for this divine service. ... So Vespasian, believing that his good fortune was capable of anything and that nothing was any longer incredible, with a smiling countenance, and amid intense excitement on the part of the bystanders, did as he was asked to do. The hand was instantly restored to use, and the day again shone for the blind man. Both facts are told by eye-witnesses even now when falsehood brings no reward.

Tacitus presents Vespasian as inspired to visit the sanctuary of Serapis to inquire about "his imperial fortune."[15] There, he has a vision of "one of the leading men of Egypt, named Basilides," who was at the time "eighty miles away: then he concluded that this was a supernatural vision and drew a prophecy from the name Basilides." As I noted above, the name evokes the Greek name for king or emperor, and so the vision of Basilides is regarded as a confirming sign for Vespasian's imperial identity as supreme ruler or emperor of the Roman Empire. Vespasian remains Serapis' chosen agent. Tacitus (*Hist* 4.83–84) goes on to explain the origins of Serapis, noting his link to the Ptolemies and that some identified him with the supreme Roman god, Jupiter.

A third version of Vespasian's miracles appears in the third-century writer Dio Cassius (died c. 235 CE). He repeats the claim that the miracles expressed divine favor

---

15. Luke ("Healing Touch," 81–82) suggests intertextuality with accounts of Alexander's visit to the oracle of Ammon, and with the Ptolemies, thereby constructing Vespasian as successor to the Ptolemies as well as a new Alexander.

Miracles, Signs, and Wonders

on Vespasian and were a means of augmenting his imperial dignity and authority ("Heaven was thus magnifying him," below). And he names the same two miracles, the healing of a man with a withered hand and of a blind man. Yet Dio removes any specific reference to the god Serapis, but adds another miracle:

> Following Vespasian's entry into Alexandria the Nile overflowed, having in one day risen a palm higher than usual; such an occurrence, it was said, had taken place only once before. (Dio Cassius 65.8.1–2)

And Dio adds the note that the Alexandrians detested Vespasian:

> Yet, though Heaven was thus magnifying him, the Alexandrians, far from delighting in his presence, detested him so heartily that they were forever mocking and reviling him. For they had expected to receive from him some great reward because they had been the first to make him emperor, but instead of securing anything they had additional contributions levied upon them.

So while "Heaven was magnifying" Vespasian, the Alexandrians were detesting him, and he was impoverishing them through taxation.

These three accounts from Suetonius, Tacitus, and Dio Cassius indicate that a key function of these miracles was to augment and sanction Vespasian's dignity and authority as emperor by indicating divine blessing on Vespasian. The first two accounts emphasized the role of the god Serapis. Serapis had been a sponsoring deity of Alexander "the Great" and the dynasty of the Ptolemies; now in succession he was the sponsoring deity of Vespasian as emperor of the Roman Empire and legitimate ruler of Egypt as an imperial province. Vespasian is divinely sanctioned and his imperial dignity and authority are augmented.

But further, for Suetonius, the miracles have a wider significance as acts that denote the healing of the empire. The years 68–69 were disastrous for Rome. The unrest increased with Nero's suicide in June 68 CE.[16] Galba became the first of four emperors before the position of emperor was consolidated in Vespasian late in 69 CE. Civil war among rival factions saw Galba killed in Jan 69. Otho replaced him only to be defeated soon after by Vitellius' troops and Otho committed suicide in April 69 CE. Vitellius, though, could not unite the disparate forces while troops in the east united in support of Vespasian. After several battles and Vitellius' execution by Vespasian's troops in December 69 CE, Vespasian emerged from the military violence in Rome as the new emperor divinely sanctioned to rule. Josephus (*J.W.* 7.66) describes the people as "exhausted by civil disorders" and as "expecting now at last to obtain permanent release from their miseries."

Significantly, Suetonius follows his account of Vespasian's miracle-working by noting Vespasian's concern to heal the empire.[17] Suetonius narrates that Vespasian returns to Rome and celebrates his triumph for his military victory in Judea. Suetonius claims that

> during the whole period of his rule he [Vespasian] considered nothing more essential than first to strengthen the State which was tottering and almost overthrown, and then to embellish it as well. (Suetonius, *Deified Vespasian* 8.1)

---

16. Shotter, *Nero,* 74–86.
17. Luke, "Healing Touch," 101.

The metaphors of "strengthening" the "tottering" state suggest a dis-abled empire in need of Vespasian's healing touch and restoration to abled functioning.

MIRACLES AND EMPERORS TITUS AND TRAJAN

Other miracles take place in association with emperors. Josephus (*Ant.* 8.45–49) narrates that "Vespasian, his sons, tribunes and a number of other soldiers, free men possessed by demons" witnessed an exorcism performed by "a certain Eleazar" using methods developed by Solomon. The Emperor Titus attempted to end a plague by employing every means possible "human or divine," perhaps evoking Serapis, though Suetonius does not explicitly say so (Suetonius, *Titus* 8.4). Luke suggests an imperial healing cult was active in Rome during Domitian's reign.[18] Revelation 13:13–15 indicates miracles or "great signs" were associated with the imperial cult, namely making fire appear and animating images that talk. It does not mention healings, but it does indicate the existence of miracles associated with imperial honoring.[19]

With much extravagant language, Pliny describes the arrival of a new emperor, Trajan, around 99 CE in Rome and the sick who seek healing:

> You towered above us only because of your own splendid physique; your triumph did not rest on our humiliation, won as it was over imperial arrogance. Thus neither age, health nor sex held your subjects back from feasting their eyes on this unexpected sight: small children learned who you were, young people pointed you out, old men admired: even the sick disregarded

18. Luke, "Healing Touch," 96–99.
19. Scherrer, "Signs and Wonders."

their doctors' orders and dragged themselves
out for a glimpse of you as if this could restore
their health. (Pliny, *Panegyricus* 22)

This discussion has identified aspects of a long tradition of miracle-working rulers that preceded the time of writing of the Gospels in the later part of the first century. I have also noted that accounts of wonder-working emperors gain some prominence around the same time as the writing of the Gospels. I have argued that these imperial traditions functioned to display and augment the emperor's divinely sanctioned power as well as to signify the healing of the empire after the civil wars of 68–69 CE.

GOSPELS

In this section I explore the intertextuality between these imperial accounts and the Gospel accounts of Jesus' miracles. I argue that the Gospels imitate the imperial interest in augmenting Jesus as a divinely sanctioned agent, not of the empire of Rome but of the empire of God. Yet while the imperial accounts uphold imperial practices and structures, the Gospel accounts destabilize and repair the normativity of somatic damage inflicted by Rome's empire. The Gospels employ a different reality constituted by the empire of God that both contests, and in places imitates, Rome's empire. Yet like imperial wonders, the Gospel miracles return a healed person not to a transformed world but to health-damaging life in the empire. I discuss Luke's framing of Jesus' miracles, then Matthew's, then John's Gospel.

Luke's Gospel

Luke's Gospel presents the beginning of Jesus' ministry with a scene involving Jesus reading scripture and preaching in a synagogue in Nazareth of Galilee. The scene presents the spirit as the *source* of Jesus' powerful activity, his *commission* in terms of the calling of Israel's prophetic figure commonly called Trito-Isaiah, and the *nature* of his activity to repair the societal and somatic damage accruing from life lived in the Roman Empire. The scene is thus programmatic for Jesus' subsequent activity.

Luke's Jesus reads from the prophet Isaiah. Verses 18–19 draw mostly from Isa 61:1–2 with an insertion from Isa 58:6 in 4:18 concerning the release of captives. These passages derive from Isa 56–66, a section of Isaiah usually associated with the late sixth century BCE after those exiled in Babylon had returned to the land. Their high expectations, stoked by visions of a paradise-like existence found in Isa 40–55, were disappointed. The prophet claims to be commissioned by God to renew their hopes with good news and announcements of liberty and release in their homeland from Persian control.

Luke's Jesus reads the words of Isaiah in the context of Roman rule.

> When he came to Nazareth . . . he went to the synagogue on the sabbath day, as was his custom. He stood up to read, and the scroll of the prophet Isaiah was given to him. He unrolled the scroll and found the place where it was written: "The Spirit of the Lord is upon me, because he has anointed me to bring good news to the poor. He has sent me to proclaim release to the captives and recovery of sight to the blind, to let the oppressed go free, to proclaim the year of the Lord's favor." (Luke 4:16–19)

The reading identifies Jesus as anointed or commissioned and empowered by God's spirit to perform five tasks, the middle one comprises somatic healings.[20]

1. Luke's Jesus is commissioned to bring good news to the poor. As we saw in chapter 1, studies estimate that some 80 or so percent of the empire's population lived around, at, or below subsistence level. Food insecurity, limited economic resources, poor health with exposure to diseases of deprivation and contamination, powerlessness, low status, and considerable stress marked vulnerable lives.[21] The proclamation of "good news" announces the establishment of God's good, just, and transforming rule over the nations (Isa 52:7). The language contests Roman imperial claims such as the good news (same word!) of the Emperor Augustus' birth[22] and Vespasian becoming emperor in 68–69 CE (Josephus, *J.W.* 4.618).

2. Luke's Jesus is to proclaim release to captives. The term "release" evokes Lev 25. This chapter details a societal transformation known as the year of Jubilee or, better, the "year of release." This transformation in Lev 25 comprises freeing slaves, cancelling debts, fallowing land, and returning land to its original owners. At heart is doing the divine will of transformation that frees people from domination and ensures all have access to necessary resources. It challenges the hierarchy, military domination, control of economic

---

20. Compare Mary's song 1:46–56; the beatitudes and woes, 6:20–26.

21. Friesen, "Poverty"; Longenecker, *Remember the Poor*, 37–59; Carter, "The blind, lame."

22. Dittenberger, *Inscriptiones Selectae* 2.48–60.

resources, and elite social control that mark Roman power and it envisions a different societal experience.

3. Luke's Jesus is commissioned to bring recovery of sight to the blind. This miraculous action, representative and anticipatory of Jesus' subsequent miracles, restores somatic and societal functions. Its inclusion in this sequence of tasks involving the establishment of divine rule and societal transformation frames Jesus' miracles as acts of release from and repair of the imperial damage that its victims bear in their bodies.

4. Luke's Jesus' fourth task—to let the oppressed go free (added from Isa 58:6)—repeats the second task and its emphasis on societal transformation and release from Roman rule.

5. Luke's Jesus is to proclaim God's favor, a phrase that summarizes the five tasks as the divine will for release from Roman rule and structures. Jesus is the agent of this favor.

This opening scene of Jesus' ministry in Luke's Gospel constructs Jesus' miracles as an integral part of his divinely sanctioned mission of societal transformation and disruption of Roman imperial structures and practices. On one hand, his miracles function like the imperial wonders in that they express and augment the commissioned Jesus' identity as a divine agent. Yet rather than maintain the imperial order, they effect moments of repair and reversal through good news for the poor, liberty for the captives and oppressed, and favor for the broken. Ironically, though, the healed continue to live in the ill-health-inducing imperial world. The Spirit empowers Jesus in this work that extends to all people (4:20–30).

Matthew 11:2–6

In 4:17 Matthew's Jesus begins his public ministry by announcing the presence of God's empire. He demonstrates its presence by calling people as disciples, preaching, and healing sick people (4:23–24). Chapters 8 and 9 elaborate this summary statement with scenes of Jesus' specific healings: a leper (8:1–4), a paralyzed man (8:5–13), a woman with a fever (8:14–15), an exorcism (8:28–34), a paralyzed man (9:2–8), a sick woman and dead girl (9:18–26), two blind men (9:27–31), a mute demoniac (9:32–34). Also included are several general scenes featuring healings and exorcisms (8:16; 9:35).

After Matthew's Jesus delivers teaching on being a mission community (ch. 10), followers of the imprisoned John the Baptist approach Jesus (11:2–6). On John's behalf, they ask him if he is the one to whom John is to bear witness. Instead of straight answer, Jesus replies:

> Jesus answered them, "Go and tell John what you hear and see: the blind receive their sight, the lame walk, the lepers are cleansed, the deaf hear, the dead are raised, and the poor have good news brought to them. And blessed is anyone who takes no offense at me." (Matt 11:2–6)

The significance of the Matthean Jesus' response is its choice of language. The language is shaped by Isaiah's descriptions of the sort of world that God's liberating presence and rule creates in contrast to the worlds created by "other lords beside you (who) have ruled over us" (Isa 26:13). In God's coming world, the dead live (Isa 26:19), the deaf, blind, oppressed, and poor are healed (Isa 29:18–19), the blind, deaf, and lame are healed and restored, as is the wilderness and desert (Isa 35:5–7), the eyes of the blind are opened (Isa 42:7). The Matthean Jesus' response evokes

Isaiah's visions of a God-blessed world. It interprets his healings and wonders not simply as acts of power, but as anticipations of this coming world shaped by God's reign or empire that embraces the marginalized and broken, repairs the damage inflicted on subjugated bodies by the self-benefitting structures and practices of the ruling elites, and manifests the will of God in the midst. Yet because this divine reign is not yet established in full and imperial realities continue, Jesus returns restored bodies to the life-damaging, daily practices and structures of Rome's world.

John's Gospel

While the miracles of Luke's Jesus contribute to his ministry of "release" from societal oppressions and Matthew's Jesus envisions a healed world under God's reign, the miracles of John's Jesus signify the nature of "life of the age," what is commonly called eternal or everlasting life:[23]

> For God so loved the world that he gave his only Son, so that everyone who believes in him may not perish but may have eternal life. (John 3:16)

The Greek word translated "eternal" or "everlasting" is difficult to translate. In English, these adjectives suggest something that is never-ending and lasts forever. But the Greek word has a different sense. It indicates an age or an era. John's "eternal" or "everlasting" life is better understood as "life of the age" or "age-ly life." In eschatological thinking, this age is not only marked by quantity ("forever") but by a *quality* of life.

What, then, is "age-ly life" or "life of the age?"

> I came that they may have life and have it abundantly. (John 10:10)

23. Carter, *John and Empire*, 204–34.

Whereas the Synoptic Gospels refer to the reign or empire of God that is present in part but not yet in full, John's language of "life of the age" refers to encountering God in the present (John 3:36; 5:24; 17:3) as well as in the full establishment of God's purposes in their future fullness (5:25–29; 12:48–50). What comprises this "life of the age"? What does it look like?

The Gospel summarizes the purpose of Jesus' signs or miracles as fostering belief in Jesus and by that means "you may life in his name" (20:30–31). The miraculous actions of John's Jesus signify aspects of this life of the age.

One feature of this life comprises the resurrection of dead bodies "on the last day" (5:28–29; 6:39, 40, 44, 54). This vindication occurs on the day of judgment on the nations and of the overthrow of the powers of evil (Isa 5:26–30; Amos 5:18–20; Zech 14). Declaring himself to be "the resurrection and the life" and overcoming death, Jesus raises the dead Lazarus (11:24–25). Lazarus appears, as does the risen Jesus, in somatic form.

Jesus' miraculous signs display this "life of the age" to comprise *somatic wholeness*. John's Jesus heals an official's son who was at the point of death (4:46–54). He heals a man who has been ill for thirty-eight years (5:1–9). He heals a man born blind (9:1–41). Somatic wholeness is a feature of "life of the age." It is typical of visions of the life of the age in which God's purposes are established (2 Macc 7; 4 Ezra 8:52–54; 2 Bar. 29:5–8).

This "life of the age" is also material or physical. Jesus' miraculous acts repair situations of deficiency. He turns water into wine at a wedding (John 2:1–11). He multiplies five barley loaves and two fish into enough food to cater a "large crowd" of about "five thousand in all" with twelve baskets of leftovers (6:1–14). Miraculously, Jesus enables some followers to catch a large number of fish after catching none (21:1–14). In each instance, Jesus' power multiplies material resources to supply people with abundant food. Plentiful supplies of food, fertility, and abundance are features of life in the age when God's purposes are established in full (Isa 25:1–10; 2 Bar. 29:5–8).

In envisioning life of the age in terms of somatic and material transformation, which Jesus accomplishes by miraculous means, John's Gospel, like the Gospels of Luke and Matthew, makes a political statement. These scenes exist in intertextual relationship with the claims and realities of imperial life. Peter Garnsey remarks that in the empire "for most people, life was a perpetual struggle for survival."[24] The miracles attributed to Jesus repair such damage and portend a qualitatively different age in which God's reign or purposes supply resources for good life for all people. In the meantime, however, healed people must resume their lives in a context of imperial deprivations, life-threatening stresses, and death-bringing oppression.

CONCLUSION

In this chapter, I have identified aspects of a long tradition of miracle-working rulers including accounts of wonder-working emperors from around the time of the writing of the Gospels late in the first century. I have argued that these imperial traditions functioned to display and augment the emperor's divinely sanctioned power as well as to signify the healing of the empire after the civil wars of 68–69 CE. I explored the intertextuality between these imperial accounts and the Gospel accounts of Jesus' miracles. I argue that the Gospels imitate the imperial interest in showing Jesus as a divinely sanctioned agent, not of the empire of Rome, but of the empire of God. Yet while the imperial accounts uphold

24. Garnsey, *Food and Society,* xi.

imperial practices and structures, the Gospel accounts destabilize and repair the normativity of somatic damage inflicted by Rome's empire. Yet like imperial wonders, the Gospel miracles return a healed person to daily life in the health-challenging daily world of the empire.

DISCUSSION QUESTIONS

1. Do you think miracles such as healings occur? If so, what significance do you attribute to them?

2. What functions do miracles stories perform in constructing the Emperor Vespasian?

3. What is the importance of miraculous healings in Luke's presentation of Jesus in Luke 4:16–19? What intertextuality exists with imperial miracle stories?

4. How do the Gospels of Matthew and John employ miracle stories in their presentations of Jesus?

7

JESUS ENTERS JERUSALEM

IN THE THREE SYNOPTIC Gospels, Matthew, Mark, and Luke, Jesus' teaching (chapter 5) and miracle-working activity (chapter 6) takes place in Galilee. Toward the end of his life, he leaves Galilee and goes to Jerusalem, the capital city of Judea (Mark 10; Matt 19-20; Luke 9:51—19:28). Here, after increased conflict with the city's Rome-allied leaders, Jesus is crucified.

In this chapter I examine four scenes that comprise Jesus' entry into Jerusalem and their intertextualities with Roman imperial practices and claims. I concentrate on Matthew's longer narrative with glances at the other two Gospel accounts. The four scenes and their intertextualities with Roman practices include:

- Jesus procuring the donkey and imperial practices of impressment or *angareia* (Matt 21:1-7),
- Jesus' entry into the city and Roman rituals of the *adventus/parousia* in which imperial officials are welcomed into a city (21:8-11),

- Jesus' condemnation of the Jerusalem temple and Roman practices of destroying temples (21:12–17),
- and Jesus' cursing of the fig tree and its symbolism of Roman power (21:18–22).

I argue that Jesus' actions coopt and mimic imperial practices and rituals while also redeploying and realigning them with God's purposes in rejecting Roman claims to world domination and in imagining the establishment of God's rule.

SCENE ONE: PROCURING THE DONKEY (MATT 21:1–7)

Approaching Jerusalem at the Mount of Olives, Jesus orders two disciples to

> Go into the village ahead of you, and immediately you will find a donkey tied, and a colt with her; untie them and bring them to me. If anyone says anything to you, just say this, "The Lord needs them." And he will send them immediately. This took place to fulfill what had been spoken through the prophet, saying, "Tell the daughter of Zion, Look, your king is coming to you, humble, and mounted on a donkey, and on a colt, the foal of a donkey." The disciples went and did as Jesus had directed them; they brought the donkey and the colt . . . . (Matt 21:1–7)

Matthew's Jesus instructs his disciples to take possession of a donkey and her colt that do not belong to him so that he can ride the donkey into Jerusalem. He instructs the disciples that if challenged, they are to assert Jesus' right to claim the animals ("The Lord needs them"). The two disciples carry out the instructions of their "Lord." Into

Jesus Enters Jerusalem

the middle of this scene, Matthew's Gospel (but not Mark or Luke) adds to verses 4 and 5 the words of two prophets from Isa 62:11 and Zech 9:9.

Both the scene's geographical location and evoking of two prophets establish Jesus' authority to act in this way. The geographical location, the Mount of Olives, evokes an expectation announced in the prophet Zechariah (chs 9–14) that on this site God the divine warrior will defeat the nations "and the Lord will become king over all the earth" (Zech 14:9). This imperial vision of God's victory fantasizes revenge on Israel's enemies. Given that the Gospel is written after Rome destroyed Jerusalem and its temple in 70 CE, Rome is an obvious target for revenge.

Verses 4 and 5 continue to emphasize Jesus' authority by citing Isa 62:11 ("Tell the daughter of Zion") and Zech 9:9. Isaiah 62 adds to an emphasis on victory over the nations. It celebrates the ending of Jerusalem's punishment in the sixth-century exile to Babylon after God was understood to have abandoned the city to Babylon's army (Isa 62:4). The use of Zech 9:9 evokes the vision of Zech 9–14 of God's victory over the nations to establish divine rule. The account of Jesus' entry to Jerusalem portends this divine victory over the nations, especially the Roman Empire after the devastating events of 70 CE. While verse 5 identifies Jesus as a humble or meek king, the context of the citations from Isaiah and Zechariah underscore massively dominating and destructive power.

The designation of Jesus as king states his power and identity as God's agent. But it is also a dangerous statement because *God* sanctions Jesus as king, not Rome. The only kings that Rome recognized as legitimate were those appointed by Rome. Herod was a Rome-appointed king (Josephus, *Ant.* 14.384; 16.311; Matt 2). Rome viewed self-appointed kings and those acclaimed to be kings by popular support to be guilty of sedition. In first-century Galilee-Judea, Rome killed kingly pretenders by the names of Judas son of Ezekias, Simon, Athronges, and Simon bar Giora (Josephus, *Ant.* 17.272–81; *J.W.* 2.55–61; 7:29, 153–55). They similarly kill Jesus as an unsanctioned and illegitimate king of the Judeans (Matt 27:11, 29, 37, 42).

But here, Jesus' authority, not his vulnerability, is on display as he orders his disciples to claim the donkey and colt. This forced procurement of someone else's property imitates the imperial practice of *angareia* whereby Roman imperial officials, such as governors and military figures, requisitioned transport, labor, supplies, and lodging from subject people. The Gospel has referred to this practice previously in 5:41 in suggesting how provincials might negotiate the cooption of their labor. That verse envisions a scene of subjugated provincials forced to carry a soldier's pack:

> and if anyone forces you to go one mile, go also the second mile. (Matt 5:41)

In 27:32, Roman soldiers compel Simon of Cyrene to carry the cross of a convicted criminal who is about to be executed.

Numerous copies of imperial orders concerning the practice of *angareia* have survived.[1] They provide evidence for the abuses that provincials suffered from this imperial practice. They also attest provincial protests against the mistreatment, and responses by the ruling power to impose what they think are "reasonable" levels of structural exploitation. From an analysis of such edicts, Stephen Mitchell argues that imperial officials and soldiers were the main sources of oppression, along with local (elite) landowners moving production to markets, and civil magistrates

---

1. Mitchell, "Requisitioned Transport," 111–12, for a list of twenty-one examples.

Jesus Enters Jerusalem

pulling rank and privilege. Imperial figures could demand "shelter, beds, food, fodder, and other necessities without payment," which imposed considerable burdens on local communities.[2]

An inscription from around the years 14–15 CE from central Galatia provides one example. It particularly addresses forms of transport that could be requisitioned.[3] Three forms of transport are named, wagons, mules, and donkeys. The inscription names officials who were authorized to seize them, payments to be made, and limits on the quantities of resources that could be seized. The second ranking provincial official or procurator, for example, could claim up to ten wagons, three mules per wagon, and two donkeys in place of a mule. Also authorized were military personnel and senators for similar entitlements. Lower-rank officials were limited to three wagons along with three mules per wagons and two donkeys per mule. Not authorized to seize transport were those moving grain or other production for their own use or profit. In addition, provincials were to provide—without receiving payment—shelter and hospitality to the procurator and his staff, military personnel, freedmen and slaves of leading officials, and their animals. The edict thus cynically delineates "acceptable" levels of oppression.

We can imagine the costly economic impact of such practices on the limited resources of local communities in providing resources of transport, shelter, and hospitality. And we can imagine the affront to the dignity of local residents and their growing resentment in having to provide food, shelter, beds, and fodder for animals without compensation. Further, this inscription, unlike some others, does not provide any regulations as to how the edict is to

2. Mitchell, "Requisitioned Transport," 128.
3. Mitchell, "Requisitioned Transport," 109 for text.

be enforced nor any penalties for its abuse. For local residents, this edict is impotent to protect them from imperial officials and curtail abuses.

Jesus' impressment of the donkey and colt exists in intertextual relationship to this imperial practice. The donkey's owner makes no appearance in the scene and his/her permission for the animals' removal is not sought. What economic and psychological impact do the animals' removal cause? What problems and obstacles do their removal pose for their owner? No mention of or provision for payment occurs. And the Matthean Jesus does not provide for their return. In this scene, the Gospels construct Jesus acting as an imperial official in imitating the imperial practice of *angareia*.

SCENE TWO: ANOTHER ACT OF IMPERIAL MIMICRY (MATT 21:8–11)

After employing the imperial practice of *angareia* to procure the donkey and colt, Matthew's Jesus is now constructed as engaging in a second imperially imitative act.

Powerful imperial officials entering cities participated in a ritual of welcome. This entry ritual, known as an *adventus* (Latin) or *parousia* (Greek), involved representatives of dominating imperial power.[4] The ritual involved a cluster of elements of welcome and honoring. It follows a military victory or recognizes the office and power of a ruling official, such as a governor or emperor. Crowds receive the distinguished person, often greeting them outside the city and escorting them to the city. Leading officials and elites of the city offer greetings and a speech of welcome that

4. Kinman, *Jesus' Entry*, 25–47; Kinman, "Parousia"; Deissmann, *Light from the Ancient East*, 368–73. On *adventus* coins from the reign of the Emperor Hadrian, Kreitzer, *Striking New Images*, 146–86.

Jesus Enters Jerusalem

expresses the city's acclaim for the ruling figure, along with invocations of the gods. According to Menander the rhetor, the speech must employ a tone of joy at the presence of the emperor/governor/general in the city, praise the emperor/governor/general, lament former hardships now past, celebrate the emperor/ governor/general's origins, accomplishments, and virtuous character, and warmly welcome him to the city.[5] The figure visits a local temple and engages in cultic activity; feasting and celebration mark the welcome.

Such welcome and honoring rituals were expensive for local communities. Yet the neglect of such welcoming rituals brought severe consequences. In 68 CE, the governor of Germany, Rufus, besieged "the city [of Vesonio] for the alleged reason that it had not received him" (Dio Cassius, 63.24.1).

Examples of this ritual abound from the Roman world.

- Ruling emperors are welcomed when they enter Rome: Augustus (Suetonius, *Augustus* 53.1; Dio Cassius, 51.19.2); Gaius (Suetonius, *Gaius* 13–14); Nero (Suetonius, *Nero* 25); Vitellius (Suetonius, *Vitellius* 10–11); Vespasian and Titus (Josephus, *J.W.* 7.63–74, 116–57); Trajan (Pliny, *Panegyricus* 22–23). The victorious general (and subsequent emperor) Titus is welcomed to Antioch (Josephus, *J.W.* 7.100–104).

- Victorious generals enter a conquered or submitting city (Camillus, Dio Cassius 6.23); the general (and subsequent emperor) Titus enters Gischala in Galilee (Josephus, *J.W.* 4.112–20);

---

5. Treatise II, "The Speech of Arrival," Russell and Wilson, *Menander Rhetor*, 95–103.

- A provincial governor such as Pontius Pilate enters Jerusalem (Josephus, *Ant.* 18:55–56) to perform his legal duties of an assize;[6]

- A victorious general returns to Rome to celebrate military victory in a triumph.[7] Pompey Magnus is honored with three triumphs between 70–61 BCE after victories "over Africa, . . . Europe, . . . Asia" (Plutarch, *Life of Pompey* 13, 43.3—45.5). Vespasian and his son Titus return to Rome in 71 CE to receive acclaim after the defeat of Judeans seeking independence and the destruction of Jerusalem and its temple in 70 CE (Josephus, *J.W.* 7.63–74, 116–57).

The Jewish historian Josephus narrates the great excitement and events surrounding Vespasian's entry to Rome after his victory in Judea and his becoming emperor. Crowds pour out of the city to welcome him (*J.W.* 7.64–71). They hail him as "benefactor," "savior," and "only worthy emperor of Rome." Vespasian offered sacrifices of thanksgiving (*J.W.* 7.72) and crowds feasted and prayed for his well-being (*J.W.* 7.73–74).

Subsequently Josephus describes the celebration of the victory over Jerusalem in a joint-triumph for Vespasian and his son Titus (*J.W.* 7.121–57). Vespasian and Titus spent the night before the celebration in the temple of Isis. Troops, senators, and other officials welcomed them to a platform to sit on "chairs of ivory." Prayers, a feast for the troops, and sacrifices to the gods precede the procession. The procession displayed "the majesty of the Roman empire" (*J.W.* 7.133) by means of artistic works, images of gods, and animals. Captives from the war, now slaves,

---

6. Kinman, "Jesus' 'Triumphal Entry'"; Marshall, "Governors"; Burton, "Proconsuls."

7. Beard, *Roman Triumph*.

Jesus Enters Jerusalem

were paraded, chosen for being "remarkable for their stature and beauty" and with clothing "concealing from view any unsightliness arising from bodily disfigurement" from war wounds and punishments (*J.W.* 7.118, 138). Massive and elaborate pictorial images depicted scenes of the war: devastation, slaughter, fire, bloodshed, destruction, captives. Spoils from the war were displayed, including those taken from the temple. Vespasian and Titus followed. The captured and paraded Jewish general Simon son of Gioras was executed. Vespasian and Titus offered sacrifices and prayers at the temple of Jupiter Capitolinus, and celebratory feasting continued.

The entry ritual of the triumph constructed Roman greatness in terms of supremacy and domination, paraded elite male "power over" and courage in battle, asserted the importance of violence as fundamental to the execution and maintenance of Roman power, and displayed the submission, subjugation, and enslavement of the inferior enemy. The pageant strengthened elite standing and secured non-elite admiration, compliance, and submission.

If Mark's Gospel was written in Rome around 71–72 CE, we may see intertextuality between the Gospel and this spectacle in Mark's rejection of rulers who lord it over others and were tyrants. Mark's Jesus seems to advocate an alternative societal vision and practice of seeking the wellbeing of others (Mark 10:41–45). Yet, ironically, imperial rhetoric also advocated that rulers serve or care for their subjects.[8] Mark's Jesus seems to criticize imperial leaders for not living up to the ideal he also advocates.

Matthew's description of Jesus' entry to Jerusalem echoes features of these entry rituals. A large crowd celebrated his entry by spreading cloaks on the ground and cutting palm branches from trees (Matt 21:8). Palm branches

8. Seeley, "Rulership." Dio Chrysostom, *Oration on Kingship* 3.55.

recalled the defeat of Antiochus Epiphanes, celebrations of the rededication of the temple in 164 BCE, and freedom from "the yoke of the gentiles" (1 Macc 13:41, 51; 2 Macc 10:7–9). And it recast a symbol that Rome had used on *Judea Capta* coins that celebrated the victory of 70 CE over Judea. Now Matthew's narrative has repurposed it to signify God's coming victory and reign over the nations, especially Rome.[9] The accompanying crowd shouted and cited from Ps 118:25–26, a psalm associated with festivals of Passover and Tabernacles, which celebrated God's victory over the nations (Matt 21:9). "Among the whole city," this entry parade causes "turmoil," a verb that suggests an earth-shaking event. It provokes questions from Jerusalem's residents about Jesus' identity (Matt 21:10–11).

While Jesus' entry employs common features of this ritual of entry and welcome, a couple of elements are lacking. The Jerusalem leaders do not offer a speech of welcome. They and Jesus will enter into death-resulting conflict in the subsequent scenes. And while Jesus will enter the temple in the next scene, he does not worship or sacrifice.

Is Jesus' entry a *triumphal* entry? Some interpreters have called it an "anti-triumphant" or an "a-triumphal" entry to suggest that Jesus was resisting, not imitating, imperial triumphs and entries. This approach claims that he rejects the self-glorification and domination celebrated in the Roman triumph by being a humble king who advocates service and seeking the good of the other, not military violence and domination (Matt 20:20–28).

There is some truth in this styling of Jesus' teaching and practice. But there is an ambivalence to be observed. The Gospels also anticipate Jesus' *parousia*, when Jesus returns in power to establish God's rule over all nations and creation (Matt 24:3, 27, 37, 39). In Matt 24:27–31,

9. Lopez, "Apostle," 35–38.

Jesus Enters Jerusalem

this return is presented as being marked by a final battle in which Jesus destroys Rome's military and empire to establish God's empire. It ensures the forcible submission of all opposition. As much as Jesus' entry to Jerusalem is that of a humble king, it also anticipates his eventual triumph over and domination of all people and creation in establishing God's empire.

THIRD SCENE: JESUS IN THE JERUSALEM TEMPLE AND ROME'S DESTRUCTION OF THE TEMPLE IN 70 CE (MATT 21:12–17)

Having entered Jerusalem, Matthew's Jesus enters the temple (21:12–17). But it is not to offer sacrifice, as with the imperial entry rituals just outlined. Rather, he momentarily disrupts the temple operations by driving out those who were selling and buying in the temple and overturning the tables of the money-changers (21:12). He addresses the temple personnel with scriptural passages (21:13). He heals some blind and lame people, addresses the angry responses of the chief priests and scribes with another scripture verse, and leaves the temple (21:14–16).

Often readers think of this scene as being like a transcript of an actual event in the life of Jesus. Here I view the scene as part of Matthew's Gospel, which originated late in the first century. The Gospel, written in the 80s or 90s, looks back on the destructive events of 70 CE when Roman troops, after sieging Jerusalem for a year, broke into the city to destroy, loot, rape, and burn the city and the temple. Various post-70 writings make meaning of this event. How does this scene in Matt 21 contribute to making meaning of Rome's destruction of the temple in 70 CE?

Roman destruction of temples

Despite a general tolerance for diverse religious expressions across the empire, and concerns with determining pious and impious behavior,[10] there is a long history of Roman destruction of temples and sacred spaces in contexts of war.[11] Some explained such pillaging and destructions to be one of the inevitable casualties of war. The first-century BCE writer Sallust has Cato the younger remark:

> Most of those who have expressed their opinions before me . . . recounted the horrors of war, the wretched fate of the conquered, the rape of maidens and boys, children torn from their parents' arms, matrons subjected to the will of the victors, *shrines and houses pillaged*, bloodshed and acts of arson; in short, everywhere arms and corpses, gore and lamentation . . . . (Sallust, *War Against Catiline* 51.9; emphasis added)

In the civil war of 69 CE between the forces of Vitellius or Vespasian with the position of emperor as the prize, various temples were destroyed. Tacitus narrates the four-day attack of four thousand Vespasian-supporting troops on the north-Italy town of Cremona. Intent on "lust and cruelty" and killing "without distinction," the attackers fight each other for human and material spoils, including loot from temples.

> Aged men and women near the end of life, though despised as booty, were dragged off to be the soldiers' sport. Whenever a young woman or a handsome youth fell into their hands, they were torn to pieces by the violent struggles of

---

10. Wells, "Impiety"; Köster, "How to Kill." Both discuss Quintus Pleminius' greedy plundering of the temple of Proserpina.

11. Rutledge, "Roman Destruction"; Ziolkowski, "*Urbs direpta*."

those who tried to secure them, and this in the end drove the despoilers to kill one another. Individuals tried to carry off for themselves money or the masses of gold dedicated in the temples, but they were assailed and slain by others stronger than themselves. They carried firebrands in their hands, and when they had secured their loot, in utter wantonness they threw these into the vacant houses and empty temples. . . . [T]here was no crime which was held unlawful . . . when everything sacred and profane sank into the flames . . . . (Tacitus *Hist* 3.33)

In Rome, in the same conflict, the important temple of Jupiter Capitolinus was burned. Tacitus is undecided as to whether the attackers or the besieged began the fire. He calls it "the saddest and most shameful crime that the Roman state had ever suffered" at a time when "the gods were ready to be propitious if our characters had allowed . . . ." Writing from a pro-Vespasian perspective, Josephus holds Vitellius' troops responsible for its burning and plundering (*J.W.* 4.645).

What motivates Roman attacks on foreign temples? Without doubt, temples, along with other buildings, are casualties of the mayhem of battle. They provide considerable material loot and booty that soldiers regarded as legitimate reward. Destroying temples also signify the depowering of the god or gods who were honored there, to whom enemy troops appealed for empowerment and protection in battle. Tacitus (*Hist* 3.33) remarks after the destruction of Cremona that the only temple left standing was "outside the walls the temple of Mefitis, protected by either its position or its deity."[12] Destruction also expressed punishment for unac-

---

12. Mefitis was the goddess whose task was to protect from malaria.

ceptable behavior among exotic and foreign groups. According to Josephus (*Ant.* 18.65–80), the Emperor Tiberius crucified priests of Isis and a freedwoman Ida, and razed the temple and ordered the statue of Isis to be cast into the Tiber river for contriving a plot to rape a woman under the guise of sleeping with the god Anubis. The Emperor Gaius Caligula planned to desecrate the temple in Jerusalem by installing a statue of himself as Zeus to punish Jews and force them to worship him because they

> alone of every race of men do not acknowledge Gaius as a god, [and] appear to be courting even death by their recalcitrance. (Philo, *Gaium* 265; Josephus, *J.W.* 2.184)

A further reason for destroying temples is especially relevant to the discussion here, namely temples were destroyed when they were perceived to be a "center of rebellion or armed resistance."[13] The Roman praetor Lucretius Gallus waged war in Greece against Perseus the Macedonian (171–170 BCE). He attacked the city of Haliartus in Boetia, sold the inhabitants as slaves, carried off its works of art, and destroyed the city. This destruction included the temple of Athena, the daughter of Zeus and goddess of war; her temple was a rallying point for inhabitants of the city (Livy 42.63.11).

Germanicus conducted campaigns against German tribes in 14 CE, including the inspirational temple of Tanfana:

> for fifty miles around, the Caesar wasted the country with sword and flame. Neither age nor sex inspired pity: places sacred and profane were razed indifferently to the ground; among them, the most noted religious centre of these tribes,

13. Rutledge, "Roman Destruction," 188–91.

known as the temple of Tanfana. (Tacitus *Ann* 1.51)

Suetonius Paulinus in 59 CE Britain attacked the island of Mona with groves sacred to Druids where some Britons took refuge. According to Tacitus' perspective, he cut down the groves and ended Druid rites, of which he disapproved:

> The next step was to install a garrison among the conquered population, and to demolish the groves consecrated to their savage cults: for they considered it a pious duty to slake the altars with captive blood and to consult their deities by means of human entrails. (Tacitus, *Ann* 14.30)

Rome attacked and destroyed temples and sacred sites that were perceived to be central to local rebellions or resistance.

Rome and Jerusalem's temple

The Roman destruction of the Jerusalem temple in 70 CE belongs in this tradition of destroying temples perceived to be centers of enemy power and resistance. The Jerusalem temple was a politicized and economic site that evidenced and negotiated Roman power in various ways. Josephus declares that the chief priests based in the temple "were entrusted with the leadership of the nation" (*Ant.* 20.251). They were not only religious leaders (like contemporary clergy), but in alliance with other elites and sanctioned by Rome, they were political leaders.

In the first century CE, the Roman governor appointed chief priests. Their appointment located priests in an ambivalent place between being faithful to their native traditions and accommodating imperial interests. Temple-centered festivals like Passover, Pentecost, and Tabernacles asserted the Judean identity of freedom from enslavement in Egypt and loyalty to God, which disrupted Rome's imperializing narrative, yet they did so in the context of submission to Roman domination. Josephus notes that at festivals "sedition is most apt to break out" (*J.W.* 1.88).

Nor was the temple like a contemporary church. It was part slaughter-house, and part bank with large secure areas in which residents deposited valuable possessions for safekeeping (Josephus, *J.W.* 6.282). The Roman governor Florus plundered the treasury before war broke out in 66 CE, causing protest, slaughter of residents, and looting of houses (*J.W.* 2.293–308).

Twice a day in the temple, priests offered sacrifices *for* but not *to* the Roman emperor. The Emperor Augustus had instigated this practice that expressed political power, permission, and provincial submission (Philo, *Gaium* 157, 317; Josephus, *Against Apion* 2.77). Contributing to war in 66 CE was the refusal of some priests to offer "sacrifices offered on behalf of the nation and the emperor"; they resisted appeals from the chief priests and other elites not to pursue this course of action (Josephus, *J.W.* 2.409–10). Politics and religion, imperial domination and subordination, permission and supervision, indebtedness yet independence, are intermixed in this complex place.

Some Judean leaders warned against going to war with Rome.[14] They emphasized that the temple would be a likely casualty. Agrippa urges them to

> Take pity, then . . . on your mother city and its sacred precincts. Spare the temple and preserve for yourselves the sanctuary . . . . (Josephus, *J.W.* 2.400)

---

14. Bilde, "Causes"; McLaren, "Going to War."

Jesus Enters Jerusalem

Subsequently, when Roman troops had broken into Jerusalem and victory was imminent, general Titus assembled leading officers to debate the temple's fate. Some argued that

> the law of war should be enforced, since the Jews would never cease from rebellion while the temple remained as the focus for concourse from every quarter. Others advised that if the Jews abandoned it and placed no weapons whatever upon it, it should be saved, but that if they mounted it for purposes of warfare, it should be burnt; as it would then be no longer a temple, but a fortress.... (Josephus, *J.W.* 6.236–40)

Josephus narrates that Titus decided not to burn the temple, but subsequently one of his soldiers set it alight. Titus tries to have the fire extinguished, but his soldiers ignore his commands (Josephus, *J.W.* 6.241–66). While the temple burned, troops looted its contents and slaughtered residents (Josephus, *J.W.* 6.271). As much as Josephus tries to protect the reputation of his patron, Titus, the narrative of troops not heeding his commands shows deficiencies in Titus' leadership.

Josephus interprets this destruction of the Jerusalem temple theologically by using a pattern borrowed from the book of Deuteronomy (Deut 27–29). The people have sinned and are being punished by an imperial power, the Roman military. God has appointed the Romans to be the instrument of divine punishment:

> the Deity has fled from the holy places and taken his stand on the side of those with whom you are now at war. (Josephus, *J.W.* 5.401–12)

The post-70 Jewish apocalyptic texts of 2 Baruch and 4 Ezra wrestle with the shock and trauma of the temple's destruction.[15] They affirm that the event expresses God's will and purposes (2 Bar. 1.4; 4 Ezra 3.27). They attribute blame to Israel for sinning against God and disobeying God's commandments (2 Bar. 77.2-4; 79.1-2). Second Baruch singles out priests for being "false stewards" of the temple (10.18). For 4 Ezra, the punishment results from sinfulness that is fundamental to humans as descendants of Adam (4 Ezra 3.25-26; 4.30). Both texts are confident that God was not defeated in this human failing. God's purposes are to establish God's reign over the nations; the temple's destruction is one step in this mysteriously unfolding plan that will vindicate the righteous (2 Bar. 82.2-5; 4 Ezra 5.36, 40; 6.55-56).

Matthew's Gospel and the destruction of Jerusalem's temple

From the perspective of the 80s-90s of the first century, Matthew's Gospel looks back on Jerusalem and the temple's destruction in 70 CE. So the narrative of Jesus' actions in the temple exists in intertextual relationship to the post-70 situation when there is no temple. Jesus' actions of driving out the sellers and buyers and of overturning the tables of the money changers and dove sellers are not acts of reform. They are symbolic acts of judgment that particularly target the temple leaders for their mismanagement.[16]

The Gospel cites two scripture passages to explain Jesus' actions and the failings of the temple leadership.

The first text cites Isa 56:7, "My house will be called a house of prayer." Isaiah 56 urges Sabbath observance, justice-based living, and a society that welcomes and includes foreigners and eunuchs. The temple is to reflect and

15. Kirschner, "Apocalyptic and Rabbinic Responses"; Neusner, "Judaism."

16. Evans, "Predictions."

sanction this inclusive and universal vision as "a house of prayer for all peoples." For Matthew's Jesus, the temple leaders have failed to enact a vision of universal inclusion.

In the second text, Matthew's Jesus directly addresses the temple leaders and denounces them with a verse from Jeremiah's "temple sermon" (Matt 21:13b): "you are making it a hideout for terrorists or bandits" (Jer 7:11, author translation). In Jer 7, the prophet condemns the nation's unfaithful worship practices, societal injustices, the temple leaders' oppression of vulnerable aliens, orphans, and widows, and disobeying the ten commandments. The chapter explains the Babylonian destruction of Jerusalem and its temple in 587 BCE as divine punishment for these unjust societal practices. Evoking Jeremiah's denunciation creates an analogy with, and thus an explanation for, Rome's destruction of Jerusalem and its temple in 70 CE. It too is an act of divine punishment on the exploitative and sinful leaders of Jerusalem and its temple.

Matthew's Jesus then performs an action in the temple of healing the blind and the lame (Matt 21:14).[17] This action, his last healings, focuses on those who are casualties of the unjust societal structures and practices of the Roman world with which the temple leaders are allied and by which they are sanctioned. Somatic ailments such as blindness and damage to limbs emerge in contexts of food insecurity, hard work, considerable poverty, and high levels of stress marked by nutritional deficiencies and a lack of immunity. Jesus restores their health, portends societal integration, and anticipates the new or eschatological age of abundant fertility and somatic wholeness.[18] He accomplishes what the Jerusalem leaders, allies of Rome, cannot accomplish.

---

17. Carter, "The blind, lame."
18. See chapter 6 above.

Jesus' act is met with two responses. Children celebrate Jesus as "the son of David." The title continues focus on Jesus' identity as a king (Matt 21:5), but also recalls Solomon, who was a son of David and was associated with healings and exorcisms (see chapter 6).

A second response comes from the chief priests and scribes who become angry (Matt 21:15).

Jesus addresses them subsequently in a parable in 22:1–10. That parable concerns a king (God) who invites the leaders (Jerusalem and temple leaders) to celebrate the wedding feast of his son (Jesus). They insult the king by refusing and killing the king's slaves or messengers. The angry king killed them and burned their city (Jerusalem in 70 CE). The parable explains the burning of Jerusalem and its temple in 70 CE as divinely initiated punishment for the leaders' rejection of Jesus as God's agent.

A FOURTH ACTION: CURSING THE FIG TREE (MATT 21:18–22)

Matthew's Jesus leaves the temple and Jerusalem (21:17). The next day he returns to the city. Being hungry, he sees a fig tree that has leaves but no fruit, curses it, and it withers immediately (Matt 21:18–20).

Some interpreters have been troubled by this scene that seems to present Jesus having a tantrum and needlessly destroying a tree. Others have interpreted it as a curse on all Israel, an impossible interpretation since all Israel is not in view. More likely, given the post-70 perspective of the Gospel, and the context of the previous scene in the temple, others have seen a curse on the temple leaders for failing to produce the fruit/societal life pleasing to God (Matt 21:12–15, 23, 45). This latter interpretation is common.

Jesus Enters Jerusalem

Another perspective emerges when the scene is set in intertextual relationship with Roman traditions. A fig tree is a central part of one of Rome's foundation myths. Under a fig tree, so it was repeatedly told, the wolf nursed the twin sons of Mars and founders of Rome, Romulus and Remus. It marked the spot where they emerged from the Tiber before the shepherd Faustulus took them to his house. The fig tree was located near a cave (the Lupercal) at the bottom of the Palatine Hill in Rome.

Numerous coins and carved panels such as on Augustus' Ara Pacis in Rome and in a first-century CE Roman imperial cult temple built by Herod Philip in the Galilee presented Rome's foundation myth by depicting the fig tree, Romulus and Remus, and the wolf.[19]

> A fig-tree growing in the actual forum and meeting-place of Rome is worshipped as sacred, . . . as a memorial of the fig-tree under which the nurse of Romulus and Remus first sheltered those founders of the empire on the Lupercal Hill—the tree that has been given the name of Ruminalis, because it was beneath it that the wolf was discovered giving her *rumis* (that was the old word for breast) to the infants—a marvelous occurrence commemorated in bronze close by, as though the wolf had of her own accord passed across the meeting-place while Attus Naevius was taking the omens. And it is also a portent of some future event when it withers away and then by the good offices of the priests is replanted. (Pliny, *NH* 15.77; also Livy 1.4.1–9; Ovid, *Fasti* 2.404–22; Plutarch, *Romulus* 4.1).

---

19. Weissenrieder, "Cultural Translation," 210–19.

Tacitus confirms Pliny's reference to the tree's function in providing "a portent of some future event when it withers away." In the year 58 CE,

> the tree in the Comitium, known as the Ruminalis, which eight hundred and thirty years earlier had sheltered the infancy of Remus and Romulus, through the death of its boughs and the withering of its stem, reached a stage of decrepitude which was regarded as a portent, until it renewed its verdure in fresh shoots. (Tacitus, *Ann* 13.58)

The fig tree evokes Rome's foundation myth of Romulus and Remus that accounts for "the founding of this great City, and the beginning of the mightiest of empires, next after that of Heaven" (Livy 1.4.5). Not surprisingly, emperors wanted to align themselves with this myth.

Octavian, the emperor known as Augustus (d. 14 CE), wanted to be called Romulus, thereby constructing his identity as a second founder of the city. But the senate and people called him "Augustus" to express his world-wide power and domination:

> Caesar was exceedingly desirous of being called Romulus, but when he perceived that this caused him to be suspected of desiring the kingship, he desisted from his efforts to obtain it, and took the title of "Augustus," signifying that he was more than human; for all the most precious and sacred objects are termed "*augusta*." (Dio Cassius 53.16.7–8)

The biographer Suetonius repeats the link between Augustus and Romulus as founders of the city:

> For when some expressed the opinion that he ought to be called Romulus as a second founder

Jesus Enters Jerusalem

of the city, Plancus carried the proposal that he should rather be named Augustus, on the ground that this was not merely a new title but a more honourable one. (Suetonius, *Augustus* 7)

In cursing the fig tree in the context of condemning the temple leadership, Jesus' act signifies their condemnation and interprets the temple's destruction in 70 as judgment on their failed leadership. But the temple does not exist in isolation from Roman power, as we have seen. It operates in alliance with and submission to Roman supervision and permission. Cursing the fig tree and its subsequent withering also symbolically attack Rome's foundation myth. The act declares judgment on Rome and portends its demise. Drawing on a pattern from scripture,[20] the scene constructs Rome, the agent of the punitive divine will in 70 CE against the temple, as a future object of God's punishment that will be enacted at Jesus' return.[21]

In this context, the repeated acclamations of Jesus as son of David when he enters the city and is present in the temple (Matt 21:9, 15) take on further importance. These acclamations link Jesus with one of Israel's foundation myths, that of King David, who united the nation as agent of God's favor and just purposes. As king, his task or "job description" was set out in a royal psalm like Psalm 72. He was to seek justice for the poor, deliver the needy, crush the oppressor, and deliver the people from oppression and violence (Ps 72:1–4, 12–14). This vision aligns Jesus as son of King David with the poor, the needy, and the oppressed

---

20. Imperial power as expressive of divine punishment in turn punished by God: so Assyria, Isa 7–9; the sixth-century exile to and deliverance from Babylon (Deut 28–30; 1 Kgs 9:1–9; 2 Kgs 17, 24–25); the Seleucid Antiochus Epiphanes (2 Macc 5–7); Pompey Magnus (*Psalms of Solomon* 2, 17). Carter, *Matthew and Empire*, 75–107.

21. Carter, "Are There Imperial Texts?"

and not with imperial domination, violence, and forced submission, at least until Jesus returns in power to destroy Roman rule. Two foundation myths, two revered ancestors, two societal visions collide.

CONCLUSION

I have discussed four scenes that comprise Jesus' entry into Jerusalem and their intertextualities with Roman imperial practices and claims: Jesus procuring the donkey and imperial practices of impressment or *angareia* (Matt 21:1–7); Jesus' entry into the city and Roman rituals of the *adventus/parousia* in which imperial officials are welcomed into a city (21:8–11); Jesus' condemnation of the Jerusalem temple and Roman practices of destroying temples (21:12–17); and Jesus' cursing of the fig tree and its symbolism of Roman power (21:18–22). I have argued that Jesus' actions coopt and mimic imperial practices and rituals while also redeploying and realigning them with God's purposes and rejecting Roman claims to world domination.

DISCUSSION QUESTIONS

1. What are the implications for understanding Jesus' procuring of the donkey in the light of imperial practices of impressment or *angareia*?

2. How do understandings of imperial entry rituals add to our understanding of Jesus' entry to Jerusalem?

3. What is the importance of Rome's destruction of the Jerusalem temple in 70 CE? From the perspective of several decades after this event (the 80s-90s), what is

the significance of Matthew's narrative of Jesus' actions in the temple?

4. What impact does intertextuality between Roman traditions about the role of the fig tree in Rome's founding and Jesus' cursing of the fig tree have?

8

JESUS DIES

THE GOSPELS AGREE THAT Jesus died on a Roman cross as a political rebel. Crucifixion was a shameful and painful way to die, and a public means by which Rome exercised its domination and control over subjugated provincials.

While the Gospels narrate Jesus' shameful crucifixion, they also reframe his death by drawing on long-held traditions of the "noble death." This chapter examines

- the intertextuality between Roman practices of crucifixion and Jesus' crucifixion,
- the intertextuality between Jesus' death sentence as "king of the Judeans" and other executed kingly pretenders,
- and the intertextuality between traditions of noble death and the Gospel presentations of Jesus' death.

Jesus Dies

DEATH BY CRUCIFIXION

Crucifixion was a feared and frightful form of the death penalty. Cicero calls it a "cruel and terrifying penalty" (*In Verrine* 2.5.165). He describes "the dread of the cross" from which elite men should be free (Cicero *Pro Rabirio* 16). Josephus notes the capture of a soldier Eleazar and the Roman commander's swift resort to crucifixion, "the most pitiable of deaths," as an intimidating form of punishment:

> Bassus proceeded to practise a ruse upon the enemy, desiring so to intensify their distress as to compel them to purchase the man's life by the surrender of the fort; and in this hope he was not disappointed. For he ordered a cross to be erected, as though intending to have Eleazar instantly suspended; at which sight those in the fortress were seized with deeper dismay and with piercing shrieks exclaimed that the tragedy was intolerable. At this juncture, moreover, Eleazar besought them not to leave him to undergo the most pitiable of deaths.... (Josephus, *J.W.* 7.202–3)

The writer of Hebrews calls crucifixion a "shameful" death (Heb 12:2). Trypho describes it as shameful and dishonorable (Justin, *Dialogue with Trypho* 90.1). Augustine (*Tractates on the Gospel of John* 36.4) observes the protracted and painful nature of death by crucifixion:[1]

> The crucified ... were killed by a slow lingering death. To be crucified was not merely to be put to death; for the victim lived long on the cross, not because longer life was chosen, but because death itself was stretched out that the pain might not be too quickly ended.

---

1. Cook, *Crucifixion*, 190, 426.

The public spectacle of crucifixion was intended to intimidate provincials and compel compliance or surrender. During the war of 66–70 CE, the Roman general (and future emperor) Titus employs this approach:

> One incident in this engagement was the capture of a Jewish prisoner, whom Titus ordered to crucifixion before the walls, in the hope that the spectacle might lead the rest to surrender in dismay. (Josephus, *J.W.* 5.289)

The indignities of crucifixion could include nudity, denial of burial,[2] as well as the crucified body providing carrion for vultures:

> The vulture rushes from cattle, dogs, or crucifixions, carrying bits of carrion to its young. (Juvenal, *Sat* 14.77–78)

Rome employed a range of methods for the death penalty, including beheading, burning, wild beasts, torture, and suicide.[3] Punishment did not so much fit the crime as the social status of the offender:

> The same crimes are committed by many people, but with differing outcomes. That guy got crucified as the reward for his villainy, but this guy got crowned. (Juvenal, *Sat* 13.103–5)

Crucifixion was commonly a status-specific punishment, generally not used for Roman citizens and elites. Cicero is horrified that the governor crucified a Roman citizen of some standing:

> The Roman people will believe those Roman knights who, called to give evidence before

---

2. Cook, *Crucifixion*, 429n69.
3. Apuleius, *Metamorphoses* 6.31.1.

you, affirmed that a Roman citizen, though he
produced respectable men as his guarantors,
was crucified before their own eyes. (Cicero, *In
Verrine* 2.1.5)

And with outrage, Josephus protests the crucifixion of
some elite men, women, and children of Jerusalem by the
Roman governor Florus:

> For Florus ventured that day to do what none
> had ever done before, namely, to scourge before
> his tribunal and nail to the cross men of equestrian rank, men who, if Jews by birth, were at
> least invested with that Roman dignity. (Josephus, *J.W.* 2.308)

Josephus does not, though, express the same outrage
when governor Florus scourges and crucifies some 630
lower status citizens (including women and children) who
had been arrested after disturbances in Jerusalem (Josephus, *J.W.* 2.306–7).

Crucifixion was particularly employed for "slaves,
freedmen, bandits, foreigners and occasionally freeborn
citizens" as well as *peregrini* (provincials who were not citizens), freedwomen, and soldiers.[4] Tacitus (*Hist* 2.72.2) refers to crucifixion as the normative punishment for slaves:

> No faith was put in his answers; and after he
> had been recognized by his master as a runaway
> slave, Geta by name, he suffered the punishment
> usually inflicted on slaves.

A slave who had escaped from his master and betrayed
the city of Tarracina to Vitellius' troops was crucified:

> The Tarracines, however, found comfort in the
> fact that the slave of Verginius Capito, who had

---

4. Cook, *Crucifixion*, 158, 160.

betrayed them, was crucified . . . . (Tacitus *Hist* 4.3)

Martial narrates the death of a criminal/slave crucified as part of the games or spectacles performed when the Colosseum was dedicated in Rome in 80 CE. His name is Laureolus and while he is on the cross his body is torn apart by a bear.

> Laureolus, hanging on no sham cross, gives his naked flesh to a Caledonian bear. His lacerated limbs lived on, dripping gore, and in all his body, body there was none. Finally he met with the punishment he deserved; the guilty wretch had plunged a sword into his father's throat or his master's, or in his madness had robbed a temple of its secret gold, or laid a cruel torch to Rome. (Martial, *On the Spectacles,* 9)

In describing this entertainment, Martial recognizes that crucifixion is the punishment for various crimes such as murder, patricide, robbery, or arson. Other references name further victims punished by crucifixion such as bandits (Plutarch, *Caesar* 2.7; Mark 15:27), insurrectionists (Josephus, *Ant.* 17.295), and women (Josephus, *Ant.* 18.79).

In his detailed account of references to crucifixion, Cook cites Aubert's statement concerning the "primary purpose" of crucifixion. Its purpose was to "emphasize the victim's final irrevocable rejection from the civic and international community and the total denial of any form of legal protection. . . . In so doing it reduced the victims to, and treated them as, slaves."[5]

Crucifixions might involve various practices; there was not one fixed performance. The accounts of Jesus' crucifixion share significant intertextuality with features

---

5. Cook, *Crucifixion*, 160.

of accounts of other crucifixions.⁶ One feature involved some form of torture before crucifixion, such as whipping. Pilate has Jesus whipped (Mark 15:15). Jesus is subject to a psychological form of torture in mocking from the soldiers (Mark 15:16–20). Another feature involves the condemned walking in chains, something the Gospels do not mention. They do share another feature, namely the condemned is required to carry part of their cross, especially the crossbeam known as the *patibulum* (John 19:17; compare Mark 15:21). The Gospels do not clarify whether Jesus is crucified naked. They do reflect the placing of a placard or *titulus* that identifies his crime as "king of the Judeans" (Mark 15:26). They specify the location of his crucifixion outside the city (Mark 15:22; John 19:20). And they attribute words to the crucified Jesus, a feature fairly rare in accounts of crucifixions (Mark 15:34). John 19:33 mentions an uncommon practice of breaking Jesus' legs. Jesus' body is not left on the cross to rot as with some crucified victims. As with other victims, his body is removed for burial (Mark 15:42–47).

WHY IS JESUS CRUCIFIED?

Jesus is crucified as king of the Judeans.⁷ What makes this a crucifiable offense? Intersectionality with other executed kingly pretenders and rebels provides the explanation.

One of the ways that Rome governed was to sanction local kings in provinces as Roman allies or "friends" or client kings.⁸ Often these geographical regions were on the margins of the empire or in areas difficult to subdue. Local kings were permitted to keep their thrones and related

6. Cook, *Crucifixion*, 423–30.

7. Mark 15:2, 9, 12, 18, 26, 32; Matt 27:11, 29, 37, 42; Luke 23:3, 37, 38; John 18:33, 37, 39; 19:3, 12, 14, 15, 19, 21

8. Braund, *Rome*.

power and privileges, as long as they represented and advocated Roman interests in their administrative area. The power dynamics were complex. In relation to Rome they were described as "friends," yet Rome held the upper hand, even as local kings expected Roman protection and support thereby ensuring mutual loyalty and some benefits.

King Herod, associated in Matthew 2 with killing the infants of Bethlehem, was a client or puppet king sanctioned by Rome. He was initially appointed "king of Judea" by the Roman senate in 40–37 BCE. Mark Antony along with Octavian functioned as patrons for Herod and advocated his appointment as king (Josephus, *Ant.* 14.381–89). Subsequently, Herod supported Antony in the civil war with Octavian/Augustus (*Ant.* 15.161–62). Antony's defeat in 31 BCE, however, placed Herod's hold on power in a precarious position. He journeyed to meet with the victorious Octavian/Augustus and argued that he would be as loyal to Octavian as he had been a friend to Antony if Octavian/Augustus would allow him to keep his kingship. Augustus agreed and Herod thereafter reciprocated by advocating strongly for Roman interests in the eastern area of the empire (Josephus, *Ant.* 15.187–99; *J.W.* 1.386–94).

Roman sanction, then, was the *only* way of gaining kingship in the provinces of the Roman Empire. Even to claim descent in a royal line was not sufficient without that sanction. Jesus, for example, is born in the line of King David, but that royal descent does not protect him from a Roman cross (Matt 1:1, 17, 20). Roman authorities understood claims to and practices of kingship without Roman sanction to be rebellion. Such claimants were executed.

> And so Judaea was filled with brigandage. Anyone might make himself a king as the head of a band of rebels whom he fell in with, and then

would press on to the destruction of the community. (Josephus, *Ant.* 17.258)

We have accounts of several figures who constructed themselves as populist kings without Rome's sanction. They attracted followers, attacked imperial personnel and property, and paid for their rebellion with their lives. One such character was Simon, who claimed to be a king. He was

> one of the royal slaves, proud of his tall and handsome figure, [who] assumed the diadem. Perambulating the country with the brigands whom he had collected, he burnt down the royal palace at Jericho and many other stately mansions, such incendiarism providing him with an easy opportunity for plunder. . . . Gratus, the commander of the royal infantry, [attacked and killed many of Simon's followers]. Simon himself, endeavouring to escape up a steep ravine, was intercepted by Gratus, who struck the fugitive from the side a blow on the neck, which severed his head from his body. (Josephus, *J.W.* 2.57–59)

In Josephus' other account of Simon, his followers "in their madness" proclaimed him king:

> he was bold enough to place the diadem on his head and having got together a body of men he was himself also proclaimed king by them in their madness. (Josephus, *Ant.* 17.273)

Another figure named Athrongaeus has similar aspirations to be a king:

> Now, too, a mere shepherd had the temerity to aspire to the throne. He was called Athrongaeus. . . . To each of [his four brothers], he entrusted an armed band . . . while he himself, like a king,

handled matters of graver moment. It was now that he donned the diadem, but his raiding expeditions throughout the country with his brothers continued long afterwards. Their principal object was to kill Romans and royalists. . . . On one occasion they ventured to surround, near Emmaus, an entire Roman company, engaged in convoying corn and arms to the legion. Their centurion Arius and forty of his bravest men were shot down by the brigands; . . . these men were making the whole of Judaea one scene of guerilla warfare. (Josephus, *J.W.* 2.60-65)

Elsewhere, Josephus comments about Athrongaeus/Athronges:

> This man had the temerity to aspire to the kingship. . . . Athronges himself put on the diadem. . . . This man kept his power for a long while for he had the title of king and nothing to prevent him from doing as he wished. (Josephus, *Ant.* 17.278, 280-81)

Another figure, Simon bar Giora, played a key role in the war for independence in 66-70. He emerged as a popular military leader in attacks on the Romans (Josephus, *J.W.* 2.521). Subsequently he "aspired to despotic power" (*J.W.* 4.508) and raised an army "subservient to his command as to a king" (*J.W.* 4.510). He captured Hebron, where, centuries before, David had been anointed king (2 Sam 2:1-4; *J.W.* 4.529). Subsequently with Jerusalem's defeat, Simon rose from the ground wearing a purple royal mantle, and surrendered himself to the Romans. He was executed in Rome during the triumph celebrating Vespasian and Titus' victory (Josephus, *J.W.* 7.29, 154-55).[9]

---

9. See the discussion of entry processions and the triumph in chapter 7.

Jesus as king

To claim to be a king without Roman sanction was considered to be insubordination and was punished by death. Jesus performs a number of "kingly" actions. He begins his public ministry by announcing he represents a kingdom or empire that is not Rome's, and he does so with divine sanction (Mark 1:9–15). He gathers followers, teaches a vision of societal structures and practices, and attracts considerable crowds (Mark 1:16–20, 38–39; 3:7–9). He does a kinglike thing in serving them with benefits such as healings and food (Mark 3:7–11; 6:30–44).[10] Some crowds consider him to be a king and want to acknowledge it publicly (John 1:49; 6:15). Others address him as "son of David" (Mark 10:48) and greet him with a form of *adventus/parousia*, the welcome ritual for ruling figures, when he enters Jerusalem (Mark 11:1–11). He attacks the powerbase of the ruling faction in Jerusalem (Matt 21:12–17), declares that he will return to destroy the Roman Empire (Matt 24:27–31), and, as king, hold the nations to account for how they have treated the poor, needy, and vulnerable (25:31–46, esp. vv. 34, 40).

Not surprisingly, in the scenes involving Pilate and Jesus, Pilate's central concern is to establish that Jesus is a kingly claimant without Roman sanction. In John's account, Pilate asks Jesus twice about his identity as king of the Judeans (18:33, 37). Jesus does not avoid nor dispute the term, but he responds by emphasizing the origin of his kingship. "My kingdom is not from this world" (18:36). This statement does not mean (as is often claimed) that Jesus' rule or kingship has nothing to do with this world or politics; his actions and teaching show that claim is false. Rather, he is making a claim about the *origin* or the *source* of his kingship. Significantly (and seditiously), it is from *God*, not

---

10. Seeley, "Rulership."

from Rome. Subsequently, the Jerusalem leaders remind Pilate of the treasonous significance of this claim, which requires Pilate to crucify Jesus. "If you release this man, you are no friend of the emperor. Everyone who claims to be a king sets himself against the emperor" (John 19:12). To claim to be king without Rome's sanction is understood to be a rebellious claim against the emperor's authority. Jesus is crucified as a rebel king.

Who you are is the company you keep

This understanding of Jesus' crucifixion as a rebel, unsanctioned king is confirmed by the fact that he is arrested as a "bandit"[11] and crucified with "bandits."[12] The term "bandits" is better translated as "domestic terrorists" or "insurrectionists" or "social dissidents." Varus, the governor of Syria, crucified some two thousand people whom Josephus names as rebels:

> Varus then sent part of his army . . . to search for those who were responsible for the revolt. . . . The number of those who were crucified on this charge was two thousand. (Josephus, *Ant.* 17.295)

These figures were often from rural areas and subjugated to economic burdens in situations of imperial colonization. Mobilized by and loyal to a local leader, they employed violence to destabilize imperial society and authority. The accounts above of the two wannabe kings, Simon and Athronges, associate them with, and identify

11. Matt 26:55; Mark 14:48; Luke 22:52. Ironically, Jesus accuses the elite alliance in control of the temple as "bandits" who attack divine purposes (Matt 21:13; Mark 11:17; Luke 19:46).

12. Shaw, "Bandit"; Hanson and Oakman, *Palestine*, 86–95; Knapp, *Invisible Romans*, 290–314.

their followers as, "bandits" or terrorists in their attacks on imperial personnel and property. As with kingly figures, imperial officials hunted these insurrectionists and, when they are caught, crucifixion was often their fate.

Felix, the governor of Judea in the decade of the 50s CE,

> took prisoner Eleazar, the chief brigand/bandit/domestic terrorist, who for twenty years had ravaged the country, with many of his associates, and sent them for trial to Rome. Of the brigands/terrorists whom he crucified and of the common people who were convicted of complicity . . . the number was incalculable. (Josephus, *J.W.* 2.252–53, author trans)

Jesus' crucifixion with bandits or terrorists confirms the imperial understanding of Jesus as a rebellious "king of the Judeans" who threatened elite power:

> Then two bandits were crucified with him, one on his right and one on his left. . . . The bandits who were crucified with him also taunted him in the same way. (Matt 27:38, 44; Mark 15:27)

Luke's Gospel identifies those crucified with Jesus as "criminals":

> Two others also, who were criminals, were led away to be put to death with him. When they came to the place that is called The Skull, they crucified Jesus there with the criminals, one on his right and one on his left. (Luke 23:32–33)

Luke's account describes Pilate's choice between Jesus and Barabbas. He describes Barabbas as a man who had been put in prison for an insurrection that had taken place in the city, and for murder. (Luke 23:18–19)

John's Gospel defines Barabbas as a bandit (John 18:40).

Protecting their power and societal vision, structures, and practices, the Romans and their elite provincial allies crucify Jesus as a bandit and treasonous, unsanctioned king of the Judeans who threatens their status quo.

JESUS'S DEATH AS A NOBLE DEATH?

One of the long-standing perspectives on death in the Roman world was known as the "noble death." This centuries-old and honorable perspective was shaped by Homer's presentation of battlefield deaths, by funeral orations, by accounts of Socrates' death, and accounts of martyrdoms.[13]

Lysias

For example, in the funeral oration for dead soldiers, the orator Lysias (d. c. 380 BCE) praises the courage and duty of the soldiers.[14] They showed themselves to be brave, manly men in battle. Their deaths were patriotic in reflecting their commitment to defend their native lands and their freedom. "They preferred death with freedom over life with slavery, . . . wanting more to die in their land than to live dwelling in another's" (*Oration*, 62). Further, their deaths were noble because they were selfless. They died faithful to their own convictions and for the benefit of others in securing their salvation or victory over enemy forces.

---

13. For this section, Conway, *Behold the Man,* 70–78, 104–6, 177–80; van Henten, "Noble Death"; Doran, "Narratives."

14. For another example, Pericles' funeral oration, Thucydides, *History of the Peloponnesian War* 2.34–46.

Jesus Dies

> It is right also to praise the strangers lying here who, coming to the aid of the people and fighting for our salvation, considered bravery to be their fatherland and brought such an end to their lives. (*Oration* 66)

They are blessed because they chose the time and mode of their deaths, "not entrusting themselves to chance nor awaiting death that comes of its own accord but choosing for themselves the finest death" (*Oration* 79). Such noble or honorable deaths were honored in memory and were to be admired and imitated.

Plato on Socrates

Traditions about the death of Socrates employ this "noble death" *topos*.[15] In 399 BCE Socrates was convicted of corrupting the youth of Athens and not believing in the Athenian gods. He was sentenced to death by drinking hemlock. Traditions assert how calmly he faces his death: "so fearlessly and nobly was he meeting his end" (Plato, *Phaedo* 59). Plato's Socrates sustains this approach by arguing that

> it seems reasonable that a man who really has spent his life on philosophy is steadfast when he is about to die and optimistic that he'll be rewarded with the greatest of good things in the world to come when he dies. . . . [T]hose who engage with philosophy in the right way are practicing nothing else but dying and being dead. (Plato, *Phaedo* 64a3–4)

Socrates goes on to argue that philosophy itself is a "training for dying" (67e) whereby the soul is freed and separated from the imprisoning and contaminating body

---

15. Droge and Tabor, *A Noble Death*, 17–51.

(67d-e). Throughout, the tradition affirms that Socrates remains faithful to his convictions, does not yield to pressure to change them, does not seek to escape his punishment, and dies nobly with courage thereby benefitting others by providing a model for them. Subsequent retellings continued to set forth Socrates' death as a noble death to be admired and imitated.

Martyrs

The noble death tradition also continues in martyrdom stories. For example, 2 Macc 6–7 narrate the martyrdoms of the elderly Eleazar, seven brothers, and their mother. The martyrdoms result from attacks by the Seleucid tyrant Antiochus Epiphanes against an identity-defining Jewish practice, namely not eating impure swine's flesh (2 Macc 6:18; 7:1). The issue for the martyrs is their refusal to "transgress the laws of our ancestors" (6:28; 7:2). They choose to die rather than violate the divinely given laws. They remain faithful to their commitments and heritage. They endure torture from the king (tongues cut out, being scalped, hands and feet cut off; 7:4) and the reality of death in a heated pan. They succumb to the oppressor's life-and-death power, while maintaining their loyalty to God (6:30). The brothers anticipate a future victory in God's vindication (7:6), a future somatic resurrection (7:9, 11), and divine retribution on the oppressor with no resurrection (7:14) and divine punishment (7:17, 19, 34–36). The deaths exhibit their nobility and courage. They benefit others by inspiring people to resist imperial tyranny faithfully and not yield or compromise (6:31). They also benefit the nation by appealing to God's mercy to end God's wrathful punishment of the sinful nation (7:32–33, 37–38).

Jesus Dies

From these examples, and there are many more, features of this noble or honorable death tradition emerge.

- Death is approached in contexts of opposition with considerable courage.
- It is a chosen or willing death.
- It is a death on behalf of a cause.
- The person remains faithful to their convictions through sufferings, pain, humiliation, and death, often with the expectation of some post-death reward or honoring for loyalty to cultural/community values.
- The death often represents and affirms the identity of a community to which the dead belong.
- The death is often understood to be altruistic in that it occurs on behalf of and benefits others in some way.
- The central characteristic—courage—is a manly virtue, though noble death is not restricted to men; women too become manlike in being courageous and willing to sacrifice their lives on behalf of and for the good of others.[16]
- Such deaths are to be admired, honored, and imitated.

The Gospels present Jesus' noble death

The presentation of Jesus' death in Mark's Gospel shares a number of these features of the noble death tradition.[17] Jesus goes willingly and courageously to his painful death

---

16. Conway, *Behold the Man*, 71; Seeley (*Noble Death* 13) identifies five components: obedience; overcoming physical vulnerability; military setting; vicarious or beneficial for others; sacrificial metaphors.

17. On the passages from Mark's Gospel, Carter, *Mark*.

by crucifixion at the hands of his opponents. Three times he declares that he must go to Jerusalem to die as well as to experience post-mortem vindication and victory:

> Then he began to teach them that the Son of Man must undergo great suffering, and be rejected by the elders, the chief priests, and the scribes, and be killed, and after three days rise again. He said all this quite openly. (Mark 8:31–32a; Matt 16:21; Luke 9:22)

He repeats this prediction two more times (Mark 9:30–32; 10:32–34). And God chips in immediately after Jesus' first announcement to urge disciples to "listen to him" (Mark 9:7).

The verb "must" has been interpreted in two different ways.[18] One is a theological interpretation that foregrounds divine necessity. This approach understands that God has destined Jesus to suffer and die as part of God's purposes to redeem the world. This view has troubled many interpreters because it has been understood to suggest that God is a murderer and child abuser.

The second approach understands "must" to refer to political inevitability. Jesus' actions and teachings in Galilee and in Jerusalem have announced the empire of God, resembled kingly actions, attracted followers, defined community norms and identity, and directly challenged the Roman allied leadership comprising elders, chief priests, scribes, and the Roman governor in Jerusalem. He has contested their imperial vision, "power over," and self-serving structures and practices.

> So Jesus called them and said to them, "You know that among the Gentiles those whom they recognize as their rulers lord it over them, and

18. Carter, *Mark*, 228–36.

> their great ones are tyrants over them. But it is
> not so among you. (Mark 10:42–44)

Jesus collides with the ruling elites in their capital, Jerusalem. The elite cannot tolerate his challenge. The empire always strikes back. It "must" strike back. Jesus does not shrink from the consequences. His death results from his resistance to oppressive power structures and a quest for justice.

In this context, Jesus courageously chooses to leave Galilee and journey to Jerusalem for a final confrontation (Mark 10:1; Matt 19:1–2).

Luke's Gospel words this departure in these terms:

> When the days drew near for him to be taken
> up, he set his face to go to Jerusalem. (Luke 9:51)

The verb "taken up" anticipates both his being "taken up" on the cross as well as his subsequent ascension to God in victory.

John's Gospel uses different images to express Jesus embracing his imminent suffering. He speaks of his crucifixion as his "hour." In the first part of the Gospel, Jesus' hour, his time to die, has not yet come, so efforts to arrest him are unsuccessful (John 2:4; 7:30; 8:20). But at the end of his public activity, he announces "The hour has come for the Son of Man to be glorified" (12:23, 27), the hour to "depart from this world and go to the Father" by means of his crucifixion, resurrection, and ascension (13:1). John's Gospel emphasizes that Jesus is not surprised by his imminent death. It is not his defeat by superior powers; rather, he *gives himself* to die: "no one takes [my life] from me but I lay it down of my own accord. I have power to lay it down . . ." (John 10:18). And his life benefits others: "I lay down my life for the sheep" (John 10:15).

In Jerusalem, Jesus is arrested, subjected to interrogations, flogged, and humiliated (a crown of thorns; a reed; spitting; mocking as king) before being crucified. Through the pain and suffering, he remains steadfast to his convictions and identity to resist and expose imperial power. That is, Jesus' death is not just *his* death. It is a death on behalf of and for the benefit of others:

> For the Son of Man came not to be served but to serve, and to give his life a ransom for many. (Mark 10:45)
>
> While they were eating, he took a loaf of bread, and after blessing it he broke it, gave it to them, and said, "Take; this is my body." Then he took a cup, and after giving thanks he gave it to them, and all of them drank from it. He said to them, "This is my blood of the covenant, which is poured out for many." (Mark 14:22–24)

How does Jesus' death ransom and benefit many? The term "ransom" suggests setting free. It is used to denote setting Israelites free from slavery in Egypt (Exod 6:6; Deut 7:8) and exile in Babylon (Isa 43:1). In this context it suggests Jesus' death sets the nation free from Roman power though how this occurs is not stated. Likewise, the Gospels do not elaborate how Jesus' death benefits others but we can fill in some of the gaps.

His death results from a "moral confrontation" with the power alliance of Jerusalem-Roman elites. It exposes the destructive ways in which imperial power deals with those who envision and work for a different world. Further, by positing that God will raise Jesus from death, the Gospels recognize that imperial power is not ultimate and is subject to God's greater life-giving power. Jesus' death and

Jesus Dies

resurrection reveal the destructive and limited nature of imperial power.

Jesus forbids his followers to imitate the imperial "power over" model, but urges them to an alternative identity and practice that seeks to benefit others:

> but whoever wishes to become great among you must be your servant, and whoever wishes to be first among you must be slave of all. (Mark 10:42–44)

His death models this dynamic and identity. It is to be admired and imitated. Jesus instructs:

> If any want to become my followers, let them deny themselves and take up their cross and follow me. For those who want to save their life will lose it, and those who lose their life for my sake, and for the sake of the gospel, will save it. (Mark 8:34–35)

His death thus functions to define the identity of the community of his followers.

The Gospel narrative employs features of the noble death tradition in presenting Jesus' death. His death takes place in the context of opposition and at the hands of imperial elites. He exhibits courage in willingly choosing to give himself to die at their hands. He remains faithful to his conviction and mission in the midst of torturous and hostile pre-crucifixion treatment from his enemies. He expects post-mortem vindication in resurrection. His death is on behalf of and for the benefit of others in revealing the death-bringing nature and limits of Roman power. His vicarious death defines the identity and way of life of the community of followers. These followers are to imitate his example in walking the way of the cross. The Gospel seems to present Jesus' death as a noble, manly death.

HOW NOBLE A DEATH?

Yet it is not so straightforward. There are some scenes in the Gospels that exist in some tension to the narrative of Jesus' manly, noble death. These scenes introduce some ambivalence to the presentation of Jesus' death.

For example, a noble death is supposed to inspire the individual's followers, securing their admiration and imitation, underscoring community values and identity. But Jesus dies without the support of his followers. Judas betrays Jesus (Mark 14:43-46). The male disciples flee (14:50). Peter denies Jesus (14:66-72). The women watch from afar (15:40-41), but flee from the tomb (16:8). Yet Jesus is not surprised or diverted by these failures. He had predicted Judas' (Mark 14:17-21), all the disciples' (14:27), and Peter's (14:29-31) failings. His predictions indicate some control of the circumstances even as his followers' desertion introduces the ambivalence of abandonment.

In the Garden of Gethsemane, Jesus' confident pose falters. Jesus

> began to be distressed and agitated. And he said to them, "I am deeply grieved, even to death; remain here, and keep awake." And going a little farther, he threw himself on the ground and prayed that, if it were possible, the hour might pass from him. (Mark 14:33-35)

Jesus' courage fails in the face of his imminent crucifixion: "distressed . . . agitated . . . deeply grieved . . . threw himself on the ground . . . the hour might pass from him." At verse 36, he prays, "remove this cup from me." Yet he submits to the consequences of being God's agent and making known God's empire, which conflicts with imperial ways: "what *you* want." This submission sets him on the

Jesus Dies

path again to his noble death, yet this struggle reflects his (momentary) failed courage in the face of a terrible death.

On the cross, Jesus cries out,

> At three o'clock Jesus cried out with a loud voice, "Eloi, Eloi, lema sabachthani?" which means, "My God, my God, why have you forsaken me?" (Mark 15:34)

Jesus quotes from Ps 22, a psalm in which a righteous man protests divine absence and God's failure to act to rescue him. What sort of cry is it when Jesus cries out? Is it one of courage and manly strength in the face of crucifixion or a cry of fear and sense of abandonment? The latter option seems more likely. The martyrs of 2 Macc 6–7 do not cry out in this way. Rather, Jesus' cry seems to be a cry of anguish and failing manly courage in the face of a cruel and emasculating crucifixion.

GODS ABANDONING EMPERORS

Stories of gods abandoning rulers and emperors create interesting intertextuality with Jesus' cry from the cross: "My God, my God, why have you forsaken me?" (citing Ps 22:1). Olivier Hekster identifies these divine abandonments as "reversed epiphanies—gods only appearing to say that they are leaving."[19] We can briefly note three examples.

During the conflict between Mark Antony and Octavian/Augustus, signs occur that portend the departure of the god Dionysos from Mark Antony as a certain sign of his imminent defeat and death. In the night, sounds were heard from instruments, from a

---

19. Hekster, "Reversed Epiphanies," 604.

shouting crowd, and from a Bacchic revelry as if revelers were leaving the city.

> Those who sought the meaning of the sign were of the opinion that the god to whom Antony always most likened and attached himself was now deserting him. (Plutarch, *Antony* 3–4)

Suetonius narrates a dream that the future Emperor Galba had early in life, in which the goddess Fortuna appeared to him expressing her favor. Galba honored a statue of Fortuna "with monthly sacrifices and yearly vigil" (Suetonius, *Galba* 4.3). After he became emperor (June 68 CE), various signs portended his demise. He had intended to adorn his statue of Fortuna with a necklace of pearls and precious stones. On an impulse he dedicated it to Capitoline Venus instead. Fortuna was not amused. She appeared to Galba in a dream, complained of being robbed, and threatened to take away his rule. Galba hurried to his statue of Fortuna to offer expiatory sacrifices on the altar but found the fire extinguished (Suetonius, *Galba* 18.2). Fortuna had abandoned Galba: his death soon followed (January 69 CE).

The Emperor Domitian considered the goddess Minerva to be his special protectress. One of the signs portending Domitian's imminent death involved Minerva withdrawing her presence. She appeared to Domitian in a dream.

> He dreamed that Minerva, whom he worshipped with superstitious veneration, came forth from her shrine and declared that she could no longer protect him since she had been disarmed by Jupiter. (Suetonius, *Domitian* 15.3)

> Hekster argues that the significance of these appearances lies in the transfer of power.[20] "Only after such desertion could power change hands." Face-to-face encounters communicated that "divine support was over, and his life at an end." For the Gospels, Jesus' experience of divine abandonment does not mean a transfer of power to another, but it does lead to his own augmented power. Psalm 22 moves from abandonment to divine vindication. The crucified Jesus will encounter vindication in his resurrection and ascension into the heavens.

CONCLUSION

This chapter has examined three intertextualities: between Roman practices of crucifixion and Jesus' crucifixion, between Jesus' death sentence as "king of the Judeans" and other executed kingly pretenders, and between traditions of noble death and the Gospel presentations of Jesus' death. While the Gospels frame his death with long-held traditions of the "noble death," the narrative introduces scenes that exist in some tension with this model, scenes that suggest moments of failing courage in confronting his imminent painful and shameful crucifixion.

DISCUSSION QUESTIONS

1. What do we know about crucifixion in the Roman Empire? How do these understandings cast light on Jesus' death by crucifixion?

---

20. Hekster, "Reversed Epiphanies," 613.

2. What is the significance of Jesus being crucified as "king of the Judeans?"
3. What are the features of "noble death traditions? How do they help in understanding Jesus' death?

9

JESUS' RESURRECTION, ASCENSION, RETURN

AMONG THEM, THE FOUR Gospels identify three events that follow Jesus' death by crucifixion. He is raised from the dead. He ascends to God in heaven. He declares he will return to earth to establish God's purposes. In this chapter I examine:

- intertextuality between Jesus' resurrection and Roman power,
- intertextuality between Jesus' resurrection/ascension and the apotheosis of emperors,
- and intertextuality between predictions of Jesus' return and traditions about Nero's return.

RESURRECTION

Jesus had predicted multiple times that God would raise him from the dead (Matt 16:21; 17:23; 20:19). After his crucifixion, the angel declares that Jesus has been raised (Matt 28:7; Mark 16:6). Both Luke and John's Gospels narrate appearances of the risen Jesus to various followers (Luke 24; John 20–21). The significance of these proclamations and appearances is that they show that the Roman political-military-provincial alliance cannot keep Jesus dead. What appeared to be a victory of the ruling alliance's power in crucifying this kingly wannabe is now exposed by his resurrection as a failure and revealed to be a defeat of their limited power. Moreover, Jesus' resurrection signifies and portends the establishment of God's new world marked by life-giving justice for all.

Roman understandings of an after-life were quite diverse. These understandings spanned a range of views: no afterlife; a kind of shadowy existence; a collective, underground dwelling place of the dead (Hades); the soul freed from the body; a happier existence or more blessed realm; some form of astral immortality.[1] Notions of any type of resurrection were rare.

Jewish understandings of death, the afterlife, and resurrection were also diverse.[2] Some expected a spiritual resurrection (4 Ezra 7:32), others a bodily resurrection (2 Macc 6–7), others an angelic-like existence among the stars (Dan 12:1–3). Some anticipated the immortal soul's separation from the body (Wis 2:23—3:4; Philo, *Mos.* 2.288) while others denied any afterlife (Qohelet; Sirach; Sadducees [Josephus, *J.W.* 2.165]). Others expected a renewed creation

---

1. Bolt, "Life, Death," 66–77.
2. Elledge, *Resurrection*, 13–129; Wright, *Resurrection*, 129–206.

Jesus' Resurrection, Ascension, Return

free of Roman rule in which all people have access to the resources for good life (2 Bar. 72–73).

This diversity of expectation reflects a larger cultural concern with theodicy in a context of imperial power. How did life under imperial power, death sometimes at the hands of rulers, and divine justice promising a better and different world interact?[3] Where and how was divine reward for faithfulness, even to death, to be found? Various groups configured the relationships of life, death, and divine justice in different ways. The Jewish writer Josephus reflects these concerns and the diverse understandings with a generalizing formulation:

> to those who observe the laws, and, if they must needs die for them, willingly meet death, God has granted a renewed existence and in the revolution of the ages the gift of a better life. (Josephus, *Against Apion* 2.218)

Josephus' important statement recognizes three understandings. First, he recognizes a sociopolitical context in which faithful death or martyrdom result from oppression. Second, he affirms, post-mortem, the certain divine gift of a "renewed existence" and "better life," often as an expression of divine justice. Yet, third, he also obfuscates by not specifying the nature of that existence and so allows for diverse expectations and debate, even as he affirms the superior quality of this future life.

The Gospels' presentations of the resurrection of Jesus participate in this larger debate concerning death, life, and divine justice. They present Jesus' death as a noble death faithful to the divine purposes and for the benefit of others. Likewise, they present his resurrection as a triumph over Roman imperial power and a statement of divine justice for

3. Elledge, *Resurrection*, 9–15.

the world. In doing so, the Gospels stand in continuity with a tradition that shows imperial power to be limited and unable to resist God's future just world.

Central to this tradition is 2 Macc 6–7, which envisions a resurrected bodily existence.[4] In the narrative context of second-century BCE Seleucid oppression under Antiochus IV Epiphanes, the martyrs, faithful to the law, experience terrible bodily torture, physical mutilation, scalping, and loss of limbs (2 Macc 7). The sons/brothers taunt the tyrant king with declarations that no matter what he and his torturers do to them, God will restore their bodies as well as their social relationships in the resurrection (2 Macc 7:9, 11, 13, 22–23, 27–29). Their resurrection will be somatic and societal. It is also political. Their "noble" suffering will ensure the end of the divine wrath punishing the nation by means of Antiochus' oppression (2 Macc 7:18, 32, 38) and will bring punishment in ending the rule of the tyrant king (2 Macc 7:19, 34–37). This renewed "life of the age" into which God raises the dead with new bodies and restored social interactions is understood to be qualitatively different from the present.

Among the Dead Sea Scrolls, several texts declare a somatic resurrection that participates in a renewed creation.[5] The *Messianic Apocalypse* (4Q521 frgs. 2II + 4 12–13) includes "causing the dead to live" along with a recreated material world that includes healing, good news for the poor, feeding the hungry, and political release for exiles.

While 4 Ezra envisions a spiritual resurrection, 2 Baruch (contemporary with the Gospels) envisions a somatic resurrection.[6] Second Baruch is concerned with the form or

---

4. Segal, *Life After Death*, 266–72; Elledge, *Resurrection*, 26–27; Wright, *Resurrection*, 150–53.

5. Elledge, *Resurrection*, 28.

6. Elledge, *Resurrection*, 28–31.

likeness of the raised dead. At first there is continuity in the form of the body (2 Bar. 49:1—50:4). Subsequently as justice is enacted, the bodies of the wicked will deteriorate in torment while the bodies of those who were faithful to the law are transformed into greater glories. They share in "the splendor of angels" and become even "greater than angels" in an existence without afflictions and anguishes (2 Bar. 51:1–16). Second Baruch envisions not only transformed bodies but also a renewed, just world. This new world is marked by abundant fertility and food, health, the absence of fear and conflicts, the presence of joy, harmony among animals, ease of childbirth for women, and easy agricultural labor (2 Bar. 29:5–8; 73:1—74:4).

The Gospels' presentation of the risen Jesus participates in these traditions that affirm somatic resurrection. In Matt 28:9–10, the risen Jesus appears to the women in embodied form. They recognize him and take hold of his feet. He speaks to them. Jesus' resurrection body is recognizable (Matt 28:9, 17), visible (28:9, 17), tangible (28:9), and audible (28:10, 18–20). In Luke 24 he walks and talks with Mr. and Mrs. Cleopas on the road to Emmaus. Thomas touches the wound in Jesus' side (John 20:27) and Jesus eats breakfast with his followers (John 21:15).

Jesus' miracles of healing and providing abundant food anticipate this world free of damaging Roman domination and marked by God's just purposes.[7] His resurrection participates in these traditions and points toward the establishment of God's rule that recreates everything. In a sense, ironically, the Gospels replicate, but exceed and redefine, Roman imperial claims to rule over all.

---

7. See chapter 6 above.

APOTHEOSIS AND JESUS' RESURRECTION/ASCENSION

What happens to the risen Jesus? The Gospels of Mark and Matthew do not tell us. In Mark, the angel tells the women to instruct the male disciples to meet the risen Jesus in Galilee, but the Gospel does not describe the scene nor what happens afterwards. Matthew's Gospel fills in the meeting in Galilee; the risen Jesus commissions his followers to worldwide mission and promises to be with them (Matt 28:16–20). But what happens to Jesus after that is not described, though both gospels anticipate Jesus returning subsequently from heaven (Mark 13:26; Matt 24:30).

The Gospels of Luke and John provide elaboration. Jesus ascends into heaven to be with God. Luke's Gospel ends with Jesus blessing the disciples before he is "carried up into heaven" (Luke 24:50–53). In the sequel to Luke's Gospel, Jesus commissions his followers to wait for the Holy Spirit to come on them with power and to be witnesses "to the ends of the earth" (Acts 1:8–11). He is then "lifted up" and taken up into heaven.

John's Gospel makes the same affirmation, but without describing Jesus ascending into heaven. The Gospel acknowledges the end of Jesus' public ministry by declaring that "his hour had come to depart from this world and go to the Father, . . . that he had come from God and was going to God" (John 13:1–3). The risen Jesus repeats the claim in instructing Mary:

> Do not hold on to me, because I have not yet ascended to the Father. But go to my brothers and say to them, "I am ascending to my Father and your Father, to my God and your God." (John 20:17)

John's Gospel does not describe his ascension.

Roman apotheosis

This notion of post-mortem ascent into the heavens is not unique. In the Roman world, traditions of apotheosis existed whereby a human hero, a dominant powerful male such as Rome's founder Romulus, rulers like Julius Caesar, and emperors like Augustus experienced post-mortem ascent to life in heaven among the gods.[8]

Conway locates apotheosis in the context of constructions of masculinity.[9] She argues that societal hierarchy was part of a greater "cosmic hierarchy" with divine masculine perfection at its peak. In this spectrum, boundaries between males and the gods were fluid in which elite males could ascend to be heroes and gods.

Romulus

There were various traditions about the death of Romulus, Rome's legendary founder. Where and how did it happen? Was it natural or murder? Some traditions associated it with cosmic signs: the sun failed, darkness descended, there was thunder and driving rain (Plutarch, *Romulus* 27). Then Romulus disappears. Elites proclaim his apotheosis or ascent into heaven:

> the multitude . . . anxiously sought for their king, the nobles would not suffer them to inquire into his disappearance . . . but exhorted them all to honour and revere Romulus, since he had been caught up into heaven, and was to be a benevolent god for them instead of a good king. The multitude, accordingly, believing this and rejoicing in it, went away to worship him

---

8. Cotter, "Greco-Roman Apotheosis," 130–53.
9. Conway, *Behold*, 35–39.

> with good hopes of his favour; but there were some, it is said, who tested the matter in a bitter and hostile spirit, and confounded the patricians with the accusation of imposing a silly tale upon the people, and of being themselves the murderers of the king. (Plutarch, *Romulus* 27)

In this context of suspicion and distrust, an elite witness named Proculus attests Romulus' ascension to the gods where he would be a beneficial force for Rome.

> [O]ne of the patricians, a man of noblest birth, and of the most reputable character, a trusted and intimate friend also of Romulus himself, . . . Julius Proculus by name, went into the forum and solemnly swore by the most sacred emblems before all the people that, as he was travelling on the road, he had seen Romulus to meet him, fair and stately to the eye as never before, and arrayed in bright and shining armour. He himself, then, affrighted at the sight, had said: "O King, what possessed thee, or what purpose hadst thou, that thou hast left us patricians a prey to unjust and wicked accusations, and the whole city sorrowing without end at the loss of its father?" Whereupon Romulus had replied: "It was the pleasure of the gods, O Proculus, from whom I came, that I should be with mankind only a short time, and that after founding a city destined to be the greatest on earth for empire and glory, I should dwell again in heaven. So farewell, and tell the Romans that if they practise self-restraint, and add to it valour, they will reach the utmost heights of human power. And I will be your propitious deity, Quirinus." (Plutarch, *Romulus* 28)

In traditions about the apotheosis of Romulus, several features of apotheosis or ascension into the heavens emerge:[10] i) the eminent man's body vanishes; ii) a witness attests his ascent into heaven; iii) he gives counsel of political significance and exhorts the people to maintain Rome's greatness; iv) he promises to be a propitious presence for Rome. Apotheosis functions politically as an act of divine approval for elite powerful males and to secure their sanction and favor for Roman power.

Cultural intertextuality recognizes similarities between details in the narratives about the apotheosis of Romulus and Matthew's account of Jesus' resurrection/ascension.

- A missing body: Romulus, Dionysius of Halicarnassus, *Roman Antiquities* 2.56.4–5; 63:3; Plutarch, *Romulus* 27.3–5; Matt 28:6, 11–14;

- Cosmic signs: Romulus, Dionysius of Halicarnassus, *Roman Antiquities* 2.56.6, darkness, eclipse of the sun; Plutarch, *Romulus* 27.6–7, darkness, thunder, rain; Matt 27:51b–52, earthquake, split rocks, open tombs, revived dead bodies walking;

- Alternative accounts/skepticism: Romulus, Dionysius of Halicarnassus, *Roman Antiquities* 2.56.2–5; 63.3–46; Plutarch, *Romulus* 27.5–6; Matt 28:11–15, 17b;

- Expressions of honor or homage: Romulus, Dionysius of Halicarnassus, *Roman Antiquities* 2.63.3–4; Plutarch, *Romulus* 27.7–8; 28.3; Matt 28:9, 17;

- Post-mortem appearance/witnesses: Romulus, Dionysius of Halicarnassus, *Roman Antiquities* 2.63.3–4; Plutarch, *Romulus* 28.1–2; Matt 28:9–10, 16–20;

---

10. Cotter, "Greco-Roman Apotheosis," 133–38. Other traditions occur in Livy 1.16.1–3; Cicero, *De Re Publica* 2.17–18; Ovid, *Metamorphoses* 14.804–51.

- Commission and promise of continuing propitious presence: Romulus, Plutarch, *Romulus* 28.2–3; Matt 28:19–20.

The meeting between the post-mortem Romulus and Proculus on the road evokes the narrative in Luke's Gospel of the meeting between the risen Jesus and Mr. and Mrs. Cleopas on the road to Emmaus.

The intertextuality between Matthew's Gospel and traditions about Romulus positions the Matthean Jesus as one who, divinely approved, founds and commissions a people to worldwide mission and submission to Jesus' teaching. It is likewise in Acts' account where the Lucan Jesus ascends into the heavens after commissioning his followers to worldwide mission (Acts 1:8–11). And the Johannine Jesus announces his return to God (John 13:1–3) after the end of his public ministry (12:44–50). He has come from God and returns to God. Just as God has sent him as a revealer of God's life, so the risen Jesus sends his disciples to continue the same mission (John 20:21).

Julius Caesar

Similar features appear in accounts of the apotheosis of Julius Caesar (Ovid, *Metamorphoses* 15). Jupiter confirms Caesar's entry into heaven after his "allotted time and his years" on earth are finished. Caesar is a star in the heavens and so can influence earthly affairs. He prophesies that his adopted son Octavian/Augustus will exercise worldwide rule over land and sea. Jupiter rules in heaven, but after Caesar's heavenly elevation, Augustus now rules on earth (*Metamorphoses* 15.843–70). Cotter explains "that the rulings of the Caesars should be viewed as rightfully authorized by heaven and willed by the gods for the good of the

Jesus' Resurrection, Ascension, Return

earth."[11] It also shows a division of powers; earthly emperors rule on earth, but not in heaven.

Likewise, traditions about the apotheosis of the Emperor Augustus affirmed that when Augustus had been cremated, a witness saw him ascend into heaven:

> an ex-praetor . . . took an oath that he had seen the form of the Emperor, after he had been reduced to ashes, on its way to heaven. (Suetonius, *Divine Augustus* 100.4)

Interestingly Dio Cassius (56.46.1–3) suggests Augustus' wife Livia bribed a witness, Numerius Atticus, to testify concerning Augustus' ascension into heaven.

> On her part, she bestowed a million sesterces upon a certain Numerius Atticus, a senator and ex-praetor, because he swore that he had seen Augustus ascending to heaven after the manner of which tradition tells concerning Proculus and Romulus.

Augustus' apotheosis is understood as a heavenly legitimation of his earthly deeds and imperial rule on par with Romulus' founding of Rome.[12]

Intertextuality with the Lukan and Johannine accounts of Jesus' ascension into heaven similarly presents him as validated by God. He has accomplished his earthly mission of revealing God's empire and life among people. His ascension signals his acceptability to God as a faithful agent of the divine purposes. Matthew's account seems to go one step further. Whereas earthly emperors rule on earth but not in heaven, the risen Jesus shares with God "all authority in heaven and earth (Matt 28:18). Such ascribing

11. Cotter, "Greco-Roman Apotheosis," 142.

12. Cotter, "Greco-Roman Apotheosis," 142–46; Conway, *Behold*, 39–49.

denotes divine sanction for Jesus' activity that far surpasses the authority and reach of any emperor. It contests and surpasses, even as it mimics, Roman claims to rule the world.

Seneca and Claudius

This understanding of apotheosis as post-mortem, divine validation for earthly activity and rule is reflected in a witty satirical work commonly ascribed to Seneca called "Apocolocyntosis of Claudius." The strange term "Apocolocyntosis" is a play on the word apotheosis, and is usually translated "pumpkinification" to denote turning into a pumpkin! The work, written around 54–55 CE, mocks the recently-deceased Emperor Claudius as unworthy of living among the gods because his rule was, at least in Seneca's view, so bad. We should note that Seneca had a personal agenda. Claudius had exiled Seneca from Rome, so Seneca certainly had revenge on his mind.

The satirical narrative describes Claudius' entry to heaven, and mocks his physical appearance, lack of control over his body, and his inarticulate speech and stutter. The deified Augustus (*Apocolocyntosis* 10–11) speaks to the assembly of the gods against Claudius, arguing that they should exclude him from the realm of the gods. Augustus catalogues the people Claudius murdered without trial. Augustus argues that Claudius is not credible as a god and that if he is deified, people will not believe in the gods. His argument prevails. The gods consign Claudius to Hades, where he encounters the ghosts of those he killed. He is punished by having to throw dice for ever in a bottomless box (gambling was one of Claudius' vices).

The satire emphasizes that apotheosis signifies divine validation for good rulers who have represented well the will of the gods. In Seneca's view, Claudius does not measure up. The Gospels employ the same logic for Jesus. His ascension into heaven, the abode of God, signifies God's stamp of approval for Jesus' ministry—his teaching, actions, death, and resurrection. Ascension denotes divine validation, a sign for his followers that his teaching and activity are trustworthy.

TRADITIONS OF RETURN

Yet for the Gospels, Jesus' ascension to God is not the completion of his work. They agree that Jesus, ascended to be with God, will return to earth to establish God's purposes in full. The Gospels use a variety of language and images for this return. The different terms do not necessarily fit together to form one neat scenario.

For example, in John's Gospel, Jesus announces that

> In my Father's house there are many dwelling places. If it were not so, would I have told you that I go to prepare a place for you? And if I go and prepare a place for you, I will come again and will take you to myself, so that where I am, there you may be also. (John 14:2–3)

What this house, this place, looks like is not elaborated.

Elsewhere, John's Gospel declares a different scene. Instead of one of welcome and hospitality, now there is a scene of judgment and vindication in a general resurrection in which Jesus is the judge. God has

> given him authority to execute judgment, because he is the Son of Man. Do not be astonished at this; for the hour is coming when all who are in their graves will hear his voice and will come out, those who have done good, to the resurrection of life, and those who have done evil, to the resurrection of condemnation. (John 5:27–29)

This is an end-time scenario, the time of judgment that leads to establishing God's purposes and dividing humanity. As God's agent, Jesus carries out this judgment on God's behalf. He is identified as the Son of Man.

The three Synoptic Gospels commonly use this term "Son of Man" in relation to Jesus' return.

> You also must be ready, for the Son of Man is coming at an unexpected hour. (Luke 12:40)

And again attributing a prediction to Jesus:

> ... and "you will see the Son of Man seated at the right hand of the Power," and "coming with the clouds of heaven." (Mark 14:62)

This image of Jesus as "Son of Man" evokes a vision from the book of Daniel:

> I saw one like a human being (lit. like a son of man) coming with the clouds of heaven. And he came to the Ancient One and was presented before him. To him was given dominion and glory and kingship, that all peoples, nations, and languages should serve him. His dominion is an everlasting dominion that shall not pass away, and his kingship is one that shall never be destroyed. (Dan 7:13–14)

In this vision, God gives "dominion and glory and kingship" to this figure described as one "like a son of man." His "dominion is an everlasting dominion ... and his kingship ... shall never be destroyed." And this authority extends not only through all time but is universal in its extent and acceptance: "all peoples, nations, and languages should serve him." This transfer of divine authority to this heavenly figure as God's agent secures the defeat of all imperial powers even as it imitates and coopts imperial power by envisioning God's rule over all nations and all peoples.

The book of Daniel does not identify this figure as Jesus. Reading Daniel several centuries after it was written, the Gospels make the identification of this figure as Jesus who is returning to establish God's reign on earth. Matthew's description of the risen Jesus as the one to whom God gives all authority in heaven and earth echoes the vision of Daniel chapter 7 (Matt 28:18). Jesus participates now in God's rule over all things and will return in the future to judge the world and will, in one scenario, destroy Rome's empire.[13]

> For as the lightning comes from the east and flashes as far as the west, so will be the coming of the Son of Man. (Matt 24:27)

Lightning indicates that Jesus' return will be visible to many. But lightning also signifies sovereignty, the rule of both Jupiter, sponsoring deity of Rome's empire, and of God. In a context of conflict, Jesus' return establishes *God's* rule, not Rome's rule. The Gospel imagines a final battle in which the Roman military is destroyed, symbolized by eagle standards that were carried into battle lying among the corpses of defeated Roman soldiers:

> Wherever the corpse is, there the eagles will be gathered. (Matt 24:28, author's translation)

Accompanying the destruction of the Roman military is a defeat of the heavenly powers (sun, moon, and stars) that were understood to sanction Roman rule. God the creator of the heavens and the earth restores creation.

> Immediately after the suffering of those days the sun will be darkened, and the moon will not give its light; the stars will fall from heaven, and the

---

13. Elaborated in Carter, "Are There Imperial Texts?"

> powers of heaven will be shaken. . . . [A]ll the
> tribes of the earth will . . . see the Son of Man
> coming on the clouds of heaven with power and
> great glory and . . . his angels . . . will gather his
> elect from the four winds . . . . (Matt 24:29–31)

The Son of Man, also designated as the king, then assembles all the nations and divides them "as a shepherd separates the sheep from the goats" (Matt 25:32) according to how they have treated the vulnerable and poor:

> for I was hungry and you gave me food, I was
> thirsty and you gave me something to drink,
> I was a stranger and you welcomed me, I was
> naked and you gave me clothing, I was sick and
> you took care of me, I was in prison and you vis-
> ited me. . . . [J]ust as you did it to one of the least
> of these who are members of my family, you did
> it to me. (Matt 25:35–40)

Emperor Nero returning

In the last decades of the first century, the return of Jesus was not the only return that some people anticipated. At the time of the writing of the Gospels, reports widely circulated concerning the death-life and return of the Emperor Nero.[14] Nero had died on the 9th of June in 68 CE. Even though his death was witnessed by only a few, there was an expensive funeral costing two hundred thousand sesterces. He was laid out in a white robe embroidered with gold. Some celebrated his death joyfully in public. Others honored him by decorating his tomb with flowers, and displaying statues

---

14. The following discussion has a limited focus. For extended discussion, Charlesworth, "Nero"; Collins, *Sibylline*; Lawrence, "Nero Redivivus"; Tuplin, "False Neros"; Klauck, "Do They Never?" Frenschkowski, "*Nero Redivivus.*"

clothed in togas. There was a new emperor, Galba (Suetonius, *Nero* 50, 57).

The historian Tacitus, however, elaborates a wide range of responses to news of Nero's death:

> Although Nero's death had at first been welcomed with outbursts of joy, it roused varying emotions, not only in the city among the senators and people and the city soldiery, but also among all the legions and generals.... The senators [and equestrians] rejoiced and immediately made full use of their liberty, as was natural, for they had to do with a new emperor who was still absent.... The respectable part of the common people and those attached to the great houses, the clients and freedmen of those who had been condemned and driven into exile, were all roused to hope. The lowest classes, addicted to the circus and theatre, and with them the basest slaves, as well as those who ... were wont to depend on Nero's bounty, were cast down and grasped at every rumour. (Tacitus, *Hist.* 1.4)

In describing various responses to Nero's death, Tacitus highlights a class bias in the support for Nero with non-elites or common folks grieving his death. This non-elite support for Nero may well be a significant factor in elite fears of social unrest provoked by reports of Nero's return (below). This support for Nero was expressed when some of "the lowest classes" flattered the subsequent emperor, Otho, by hailing him as Nero. Otho

> made no sign of dissent; on the contrary ... he even made use of that surname in his commissions and his first letters to some of the governors of the provinces. Certain it is he suffered Nero's busts and statues to be set up again ....
> (Suetonius, *Otho* 7)

Yet despite all these public recognitions of Nero's death, some believed Nero was alive. He died young, aged thirty-one, and unexpectedly. Some ruling figures produced

> edicts, as if he was still alive and would shortly return and deal destruction to his enemies. (Suetonius, *Nero* 57)

And Tacitus narrates how in the year 69 CE

> Achaia and Asia were terrified by a false rumour of Nero's arrival. The reports with regard to his death had been varied, and therefore many people imagined and believed that he was alive. The fortunes and attempts of other pretenders we shall tell as we proceed; but at this time, a slave from Pontus or, as others have reported, a freedman from Italy, who was skilled in playing on the cithara and in singing, gained the readier belief in his deceit through these accomplishments and his resemblance to Nero. (Tacitus, *Hist.* 2.8)

This Nero-look-alike gained numerous followers, set sail, landed in a storm on the island of Cythnus, recruited soldiers, robbed merchants, and armed slaves. A centurion called Sisenna escaped the island and spread alarm far and wide:

> Many came eagerly forward at the famous name, prompted by their desire for a change and their hatred of the present situation. The fame of the pretender was increasing from day to day when a chance shattered it. (Tacitus, *Hist.* 2.8–9)

This "chance" intervention took the form of a governor on his way to his provinces who attacked the pretender and killed him.

Some twenty years later, around 88 CE, Dio Chrysostom provides some comments about Nero's death.

Jesus' Resurrection, Ascension, Return

> Indeed the truth about this has not come out even yet; for so far as the rest of his subjects were concerned, there was nothing to prevent his continuing to be Emperor for all time, seeing that even now everybody wishes he were still alive. And the great majority do believe that he is, although in a certain sense he has died not once but often along with those who had been firmly convinced that he was still alive. (*Oration* 21.10)

Dio Chrysostom confirms that uncertainties about Nero's death continued even twenty years after Nero's death. Further, his death was a surprise for many who thought (with exaggeration) he could be emperor for a long time. Moreover, the comment that "everybody wishes he were still alive" seems to assume both some general dis-ease with the oppressive rule of the Emperor Domitian, as well as Dio's personal hostility to Domitian, who had exiled him some six years previously from Rome, Italy and his home province of Bithynia. Chrysostom's fourth comment is that "the great majority" believe Nero is alive, though he had died. Suetonius reports that astronomers had predicted that Nero would fall from power but have a kingdom in the east and he would "shortly return and deal destruction to his enemies" (Suetonius, *Nero* 40; 57).

Chrysostom's final comment is cryptic and somewhat puzzling: Nero "has died not once but often." Most interpreters understand this comment to refer to three Nero impersonators that appeared between 69 and 88 with significant disruptive impact. The first was the unnamed Nero-look-alike, who terrified the provinces of Achaea and Asia, rallied supporters, and was killed in 69 CE. A second figure named Terentius Maximus appeared in the reign of Titus (79–81 CE). He recruited supporters in Asia and headed east to Parthia where he gained the support of Artabanus, a pretender to the Parthian throne who opposed Emperor Titus because Titus had not supported his bid to become Parthian king. A third figure appeared around 88 CE who also garnered support from the Parthians in the east. These last two figures perhaps enact the prediction of some astrologers that Nero would appear and have a kingdom in the east (Suetonius, *Nero* 47). And their actions and alliance with the Parthians suggest hostility toward the Flavian emperors in Rome.

Another passage from around late in the first century repeats expectations about Nero's return to Rome after his flight to the east. The passage refers to the civil wars of the year of four emperors of 68–69 CE from which the Flavian Vespasian emerges victorious. Then Nero will return from the east and attack Rome.

> Then a great king [Nero] will flee from Italy like a runaway slave, unseen and unheard over the channel of the Euphrates [Parthia]. . . . When he runs away, beyond the Parthian land, many will bloody the ground for the throne of Rome [the wars of 68–69 CE; Titus attacks Jerusalem]. Then the strife of war being aroused will come to the west, and the fugitive from Rome will also come, brandishing a great spear, having crossed the Euphrates with many myriads. (*Sibylline Oracles* 4.119–24, 137–39)[15]

Nero is envisioned as returning with military forces to attack Rome ruled by Flavian emperors, Vespasian, Titus, and Domitian.

Expectations for Nero's post-mortem return and the phenomenon of Nero impersonators attests popular affection, at least among some, for the dead/alive Nero. It also channels some disgruntlement with the status quo, first the

15. Collins, "Sibylline Oracles," 387.

Jesus' Resurrection, Ascension, Return

civil wars of 69 with no clear or stable successor and then, with the passing of several decades, the reigns of the Flavian Emperors Titus and Domitian. Moreover, the expectations and impersonations pose a threat to the status quo. They threaten to undermine and disrupt the status quo bringing benefits to some and loss to others.[16]

Interesting intertextualities between expectations for Jesus' return and Nero's return, both differences and similarities, emerge. Jesus returns from heaven with God (clearly in Luke and John's Gospels, assumed in Mark and Matthew). Nero is not said to ascend into heaven. Instead, his return is understood in geographical terms to be from the east, nearer to Rome (Archaea, Asia) or further from Parthia. Both returns involve pretenders, at least three Neros between 69–88 CE, and "many" Christs: "Many will come in my name and say 'I am he!' and they will lead many astray" (Mark 13:6). Both returning figures have supporters.

More important, both returns pose challenges to the status quo. Nero's returns threaten more chaos in the instabilities of 69 CE and the following decades in destabilizing the reigns of the Flavian emperors, especially if alliances with Parthian military power are in play. And the danger is not only to Rome; the provinces of Achaea and Asia are involved as well as provinces in the east. Yet Nero's return does not overthrow the empire. If successful, it dethrones some and empowers others while leaving the status quo of imperial structures and elite privileges untouched.

Jesus' return poses challenges to the imperial status quo. His return is also constructed as the replacement of one emperor by another. It ends Roman power and its empire as he depowers Rome's military and heavenly sponsoring deities. At his return, he establishes God's empire that comprises God's rule over heaven and earth, marked by

16. Turpin, "False Neros," 390–91.

justice, abundant fertility, good health, and harmonious interactions. It is also marked by intolerance for and judgment of any dissenters who do not join the divine program.

CONCLUSION

Intersectionality between Jesus' resurrection, ascension, and return with Roman power, apotheosis, and Nero's return highlights elements of both imitation and contest. Jesus' resurrection displays the limits of Roman power that cannot keep God's agent dead in the face of God's life-giving power. His ascension into the heavens, like the apotheosis of Roman emperors, signifies divine approval for his activity. His return from the heavens to earth, unlike Nero's anticipated return from the east, destroys Roman power and effects the establishment of God as emperor.

DISCUSSION QUESTIONS

1. What is the significance of Jesus' resurrection in the context of Roman power and divine justice?

2. What is apotheosis? How and to what extent does intertextuality between apotheosis traditions and Jesus' resurrection provide understanding of the latter?

3. In what ways are expectations of Jesus' return and of the Emperor Nero's "return" similar and different?

10

CONCLUSION

IN THE PREVIOUS CHAPTERS I have outlined intertextualities between eight features of the Gospels and some structures and practices of the Roman imperial world. I have examined the Gospels as ancient biographies (ch. 2), stories of origins of heroes (ch. 3), predictions of greatness (ch. 4), Jesus as a teacher of societal visions (ch. 5), Jesus as a worker of wonders (ch. 6), Jesus' entry into Jerusalem (ch. 7), Jesus' noble but flawed death (ch. 8), and Jesus' resurrection, ascension/apotheosis, and return (ch. 9). Attention to intertextualities have highlighted dynamics of participation in the imperial world, imitation, and contest of its structures and practices.

Why should we bother with such explorations and intertextualities?

A first factor concerns what we might call a reading strategy. Often the Gospels are read as spiritual texts, restricted to matters of personal and individual religion. As spiritual texts they are often understood by contemporary readers as concerning an individual's spiritual and

Conclusion

individual relationship with God. Often this approach isolates Gospels from everyday matters and practices, from societal structures and political practices. Identifying the intertextualities that I have outlined in the previous chapters alerts us to the Gospels as documents of political import. These intertextualities expand our horizons and disrupt spiritualizing reading strategies. They frame the Gospels as concerned with power structures, societal practices, leadership, social relationships, beneficiaries and casualties, who has access to and who is excluded from good resources of food, healthcare, housing, safety, and justice. The Gospels envision a different world and different priorities.

This recognition of the politically embedded and invested nature of the Gospels leads to a second insight. This insight challenges contemporary readers of the Gospels, whether we identify ourselves as followers of Jesus or believers in God or not. Again it is a reading strategy, to use our imaginations to build a bridge from the past to the present. When the Gospels are read in relation to political practices and societal structures, they provoke us to think not just about the ancient world but also about our own world, about our own political practices, our own societal structures, leaders, and worldviews. Who benefits? Who gets hurt? Who is excluded? Who is privileged? Who has access to resources and opportunities for a rewarding and fulfilling life? What is justice and for whom?

The Gospels read as politically embedded and invested texts provoke us as contemporary readers not to stay in the ancient world but to reflect on our own worlds, to imagine their healing, and to live toward that end.

BIBLIOGRAPHY

Aldrete, Gregory. *Daily Life in the Roman City: Rome, Pompeii, Ostia.* Norman, OK: University of Oklahoma Press, 2004.
Aldrete, Gregory, and David Mattingly. "Feeding the City: The Organization, Operation, and Scale of the Supply System for Rome." In *Life, Death, and Entertainment in the Roman Empire*, edited by David Potter and David Mattingly, 171–204. Ann Arbor, MI: University of Michigan Press, 1999.
Alkier, Stefan. "Intertextuality and the Semiotics of Biblical Texts." In *Reading the Bible Intertextually*, edited by Richard Hays, Stefan Alkier and Leroy Huizenga, 3–21. Waco, TX: Baylor University Press, 2009.
Allen, Graham. *Intertextuality.* London: Routledge, 2000.
Avery-Peck, Alan J. "The Galilean Charismatic and Rabbinic Piety: The Holy Man in the Talmudic Literature." In *The Historical Jesus in Context,* edited by Amy-Jill Levine, Dale Allison, and John Dominic Crossan, 149–65. Princeton: Princeton University Press, 2006.
Beard, Mary. *The Roman Triumph.* Cambridge: Harvard University Press, 2007.
Betcher, Sharon V. "Disability and the Terror of the Miracle Tradition." In *Miracles Revisited: New Testament Miracle Stories and Their Concepts of Reality,* edited by Stefan Alkier and Annette Weissenrieder, 161–81. Berlin: de Gruyter, 2013.

Bibliography

Bilde, Per. "The Causes of the Jewish War according to Josephus." *Journal for the Study of Judaism in the Persian, Hellenistic, and Roman Period* 10 (1979) 179–202.

Billings, Bradly. "'At the Age of 12': The Boy Jesus in the Temple (Luke 2:41–52), The Emperor Augustus, and the Social Setting of the Third Gospel." *Journal of Theological Studies* 60 (2009) 70–89.

Boatwright, Mary T. "Plancia Magna of Perge: Women's Roles and Status in Roman Asia Minor." In *Women's History and Ancient History*, edited by Sarah Pomeroy, 249–72. Chapel Hill, NC: University of North Carolina Press, 1991.

Bolt, Peter. "Life, Death, and the Afterlife in the Greco-Roman World." In *Life in the Face of Death: The Resurrection Message of the New Testament*, edited by Richard Longenecker, 51–79. Grand Rapids: Eerdmans, 1998.

Bradley, Keith R. "Introduction." *Suetonius Vol. 1*. Loeb Classical Library. Cambridge: Harvard University Press, 1998.

Braund, D. *Rome and the Friendly King: The Character of Client Kingship*. London: Routledge, 2013.

Brunt, Peter. "The Roman Mob." *Past and Present* 35 (1966) 3–27.

Burridge, Richard. *What Are the Gospels? A Comparison with Graeco-Roman Biography*. 2nd ed. Grand Rapids: Eerdmans, 2004.

Burton, G. P. "Proconsuls, Assizes, and the Administration of Justice under the Empire." *Journal of Roman Studies* 65 (1975) 92–106.

Carter, Warren. "Are There Imperial Texts in the Class? Intertextual Eagles and Matthean Eschatology as 'Lights Out' Time for Imperial Rome (Matt 24:27–31)." *Journal of Biblical Literature* 122 (2003) 467–87.

———. "'The blind, lame, and paralyzed' (John 5:3): John's Gospel, Disability Studies, and Postcolonial Perspectives." In *Disability Studies and Biblical Literature*, edited by Candida Moss and Jeremy Schipper, 128–50. New York: Palgrave MacMillan, 2011.

———. "God as 'Father' in Matthew: Imperial Intersections." In *Finding a Woman's Place: Essays in Honor of Carolyn Osiek*, edited by David Balch and Jason Lamoreaux, 81–102. Eugene, OR: Pickwick, 2011.

———. *John and Empire: Initial Explorations*. London: T. &T. Clark, 2008.

———. *John: Storyteller, Interpreter, Evangelist*. Peabody, MA: Hendrickson, 2006.

———. *Mark*. Wisdom Commentary 42. Collegeville, MN: Liturgical, 2019.

Bibliography

———. *Matthew and Empire: Initial Explorations.* Harrisburg, PA: Trinity, 2001.

———. *Matthew and the Margins: A Sociopolitical and Religious Reading.* Maryknoll, NY: Orbis, 2000.

———. *Matthew: Storyteller, Interpreter, Evangelist.* Peabody, MA: Hendrickson, 2004.

Charlesworth, Martin P. "Nero: Some Aspects." *Journal of Roman Studies* 40 (1950) 69–76.

Collins, John J. *The Sibylline Oracles of Egyptian Judaism.* Society of Biblical Literature Dissertation Series 13. Missoula, MT: Scholars, 1974.

———. "Sibylline Oracles." In *The Old Testament Pseudepigrapha.* Vol. 1, edited by James H. Charlesworth, 317–472. Garden City, NY: Doubleday, 1983.

Conway, Colleen M. *Behold the Man: Jesus and Greco-Roman Masculinity.* Oxford: Oxford University Press, 2008.

Cook, John G. *Crucifixion in the Mediterranean World.* Wissenschaftliche Untersuchungen zum Neuen Testament 327. Tübingen: Mohr Siebeck, 2014.

Cooley, Alison E., and M. G. L. Cooley. *Pompeii and Herculaneum.* 2nd ed. London: Routledge, 2014.

Cotter, Wendy. "Greco-Roman Apotheosis Traditions and the Resurrection Appearances in Matthew." In *The Gospel of Matthew in Current Study*, edited by David Aune, 127–53. Grand Rapids: Eerdmans, 2001.

———. *Miracles in Greco-Roman Antiquity: A Sourcebook for the Study of New Testament Miracle Stories.* London: Routledge, 1999.

———. "Miracle Stories: The God Asclepius, the Pythagorean Philosophers, and the Roman Rulers." In *The Historical Jesus in Context*, edited by Amy-Jill Levine, Dale Allison, and John Dominic Crossan, 166–78. Princeton: Princeton University Press, 2006.

Crossan, John Dominic. "Roman Imperial Theology." In *In the Shadow of Empire: Reclaiming the Bible as a History of Faithful Resistance*, edited by Richard Horsley, 59–73. Louisville, KY: Westminster John Knox, 2008.

Deissmann, Gustav Adolf. *Light from the Ancient East.* New York: Harper and Brothers, 1922.

Dittenberger, Wilhelm, ed. *Orientis Graecae Inscriptiones Selectae*, 2 vols. 2:48–60. Hildesheim, Germany: Olms, 1960.

Bibliography

Dodson, Derek S. *Reading Dreams: An Audience-Critical Approach to the Dreams in the Gospel of Matthew.* Library of New Testament Studies 397. London: T. & T. Clark, 2009.

Doran, Robert. "Narratives of Noble Death." In *The Historical Jesus in Context*, edited by Amy-Jill Levine, Dale Allison, and John Dominic Crossan, 385–99. Princeton: Princeton University Press, 2006.

Dowling, Melissa B. *Clemency and Cruelty in the Roman World.* Ann Arbor, MI: University of Michigan Press, 2006.

Droge, Arthur J., and James Tabor. *A Noble Death: Suicide and Martyrdom among Christians and Jews in Antiquity.* San Francisco: HarperSan Francisco, 1992.

Duling, Denis. "Solomon, Exorcism, and the Son of David." *Harvard Theological Review* 68 (1975) 235–52.

Edelstein, Emma J., and Ludwig Edelstein. *Asclepius.* 2 vols. Baltimore: The Johns Hopkins Press, 1945.

Elledge, Casey. *Resurrection of the Dead in Early Judaism 200 BCE–CE 200.* Oxford: Oxford University Press, 2017.

Elliott, Neil. *The Arrogance of Nations: Reading Romans in the Shadow of Empire.* Minneapolis: Fortress, 2008.

Evans, Craig. "Predictions of the Destruction of the Herodian Temple in the Pseudepigrapha, Qumran Scrolls, and Related Texts." *Journal for the Study of the Pseudepigrapha* 10 (1992) 89–147.

Fagan, Garrett. "Violence in Roman Social Relations." In *The Oxford Handbook of Social Relations in the Roman World*, edited by Michael Peachin, 467–95. Oxford: Oxford University Press, 2011.

Frenschkowski, Marco. "*Nero Redivivus* as a Subject of Early Christian Arcane Teaching." In *People under Power: Early Jewish and Christian Responses to the Roman Empire*, edited by Michael Labahn and Outi Lehtipuu, 229–48. Amsterdam: Amsterdam University Press, 2015.

Frier, Bruce. "Roman Demography." In *Life, Death, and Entertainment in the Roman Empire*, edited by David Potter and David Mattingly, 85–109. Ann Arbor, MI: University of Michigan Press, 1999.

Friesen, Steven J. "Poverty in Pauline Studies: Beyond the So-Called New Consensus." *Journal for the Study of the New Testament* 26 (2004) 323–61.

Garnsey, Peter. *Food and Society in Classical Antiquity.* Cambridge: Cambridge University Press, 1999.

Bibliography

Hanson, Ann. "The Roman Family." In *Life, Death, and Entertainment in the Roman Empire*, edited by David Potter and David Mattingly, 19–66. Ann Arbor, MI: University of Michigan Press, 1999.

Hanson, K. C., and Douglas Oakman. *Palestine in the Time of Jesus: Social Structures and Social Conflicts*. Minneapolis: Fortress, 1998.

Harris, William V. "Roman Opinions about the Truthfulness of Dreams." *Journal of Roman Studies* 93 (2003) 18–34.

Harrison, James R. "Augustan Rome and the Body of Christ: A Comparison of the Social Vision of the *Res Gestae* and Paul's Letter to the Romans." *Harvard Theological Review* 106 (2013) 1–36.

Hekster, Olivier. "Descendants of Gods: Legendary Genealogies in the Roman Empire." In *Impact of Imperial Rome on Religions, Ritual and Religious Life in the Roman Empire: Proceedings from the Fifth Workshop of the International Network Impact of Empire*, edited by Lukas de Blois, 24–35. Leiden: Brill, 2005.

———. "Reversed Epiphanies: Roman Emperors Deserted by Gods." *Mnemosyne* 63.4 (2010) 601–15.

Huebner, Sabine. *Papyri and the Social World of the New Testament*. Cambridge: Cambridge University Press, 2019.

Hutton, M., and W. Peterson. *Tacitus: Agricola, Germania, Dialogus*. 1914. Reprint, Cambridge: Harvard University Press, 1970.

Kinman, Brent. *Jesus' Entry into Jerusalem in the Context of Lukan Theology and the Politics of His Day*. Leiden: Brill, 1995.

———. "Jesus' 'Triumphal Entry' in the Light of Pilate's." *New Testament Studies* 40 (1994) 442–48.

———. "Parousia, Jesus' 'A-Triumphal' Entry, and the Fate of Jerusalem (Luke 19:28–44)." *Journal of Biblical Literature* 118 (1999) 279–94.

Kirschner, Robert. "Apocalyptic and Rabbinic Responses to the Destruction of 70." *Harvard Theological Review* 78 (1985) 27–46.

Klauck, Hans-Josef. "Do They Never Come Back? 'Nero Redivivus' and the Apocalypse of John." *Catholic Biblical Quarterly* 63 (2001) 683–98.

Knapp, Robert. *Invisible Romans*. Cambridge: Harvard University Press, 2011.

Kochenash, Michael. *Roman Self-Representation and the Lukan Kingdom of God*. Lanham, MD: Lexington/Fortress Academic, 2020.

Köster, Isabel. "How to Kill a Roman Villain: The Deaths of Quintus Pleminius." *The Classical Journal* 109 (2014) 309–32.

Bibliography

Kreitzer, Larry J. *Striking New Images: Roman Imperial Coinage and the New Testament World.* Journal for the Study of the New Testament Supplement Series 134. Sheffield, UK: Sheffield Academic Press, 1996.

Kurz, William. "Luke 3:23–38 and Greco-Roman and Biblical Genealogies." In *Luke-Acts; New Perspectives from the Society of Biblical Literature Seminar*, edited by Charles Talbert, 169–87. New York: Crossroad, 1984.

Lavery, Gerard B. "Training, Trade, and Trickery: Three Lawgivers in Plutarch." *The Classical World* 67 (1974) 369–81.

Lawrence, John M. "Nero Redivivus." *Fides et Historia* 11 (1978) 54–66.

Leander, Hans. *The Discourses of Empire: The Gospel of Mark from Postcolonial Perspectives.* Atlanta: Society of Biblical Literature, 2013.

Leppin, Hartmut. "Imperial Miracles and Elitist Discourses." In *Miracles Revisited: New Testament Miracle Stories and Their Concepts of Reality*, edited by Stefan Alkier and Annette Weissenrieder, 233–48. Berlin: de Gruyter, 2013.

Litwa, M. David. *How the Gospels Became History: Jesus and the Mediterranean Myths.* New Haven: Yale University Press, 2019.

Longenecker, Bruce W. *Remember the Poor: Paul, Poverty, and the Greco-Roman World.* Grand Rapids: Eerdmans, 2010.

Lopez, Davina C. *Apostle to the Conquered: Reimagining Paul's Mission.* Minneapolis: Fortress, 2008.

Luke, Trevor S. "A Healing Touch for Empire: Vespasian's Wonders in Domitianic Rome." *Greece and Rome* 57 (2010) 77–106.

MacMullen, Ramsay. *Roman Social Relations 50 B.C. to A.D. 284.* New Haven: Yale University Press, 1974.

Marshall, A. J. "Governors on the Move." *Phoenix* 20 (1966) 231–46.

McLaren, James S. "Going to War against Rome: The Motivation of the Jewish Rebels." In *The Jewish Revolt against Rome: Interdisciplinary Perspectives*, edited by Mladen Popovíc, 129–53. Leiden: Brill, 2011.

Miles, Richard. "Communicating Culture, Identity and Power." In *Experiencing Rome: Culture, Identity and Power in the Roman Empire,* edited by Janet Huskinson, 29–62. London: Routledge, 2000.

Mitchell, Stephen. "Requisitioned Transport in the Roman Empire: A New Inscription from Pisidia." *Journal of Roman Studies* 66 (1976) 106–31.

Bibliography

Moyise, Steve. "Intertextuality and the Study of the Old Testament in the New Testament." In *The Old Testament in the New Testament: Essays in Honor of J. L. North*, edited by Steve Moyise, 14–41. Journal for the Study of the New Testament Supplement Series 189. Sheffield, UK: Sheffield Academic Press, 2000.

Neusner, Jacob. "Judaism in the Time of Crisis: Four Responses to the Destruction of the Second Temple." *Judaism* 21 (1972) 313–27.

Peppard, Michael. *The Son of God in the Roman World: Divine Sonship and Its Social and Political Context*. Oxford: Oxford University Press, 2011.

Russell, D. A., and N. G. Wilson. *Menander Rhetor*. Oxford: Clarendon, 1981.

Rutledge, Steven H. "The Roman Destruction of Sacred Sites." *Historia: Zeitschrift für Alte Geschichte* 56 (2007) 179–95.

Scheid, John. "*genius*." In *The Oxford Classical Dictionary*, edited by Simon Hornblower and Antony Spawforth, 630. Oxford: Oxford University Press, 1999.

Scherrer, Stephen. "Signs and Wonders in the Imperial Cult: A New Look at a Roman Religious Institution in the Light of Rev 13:13–15." *Journal of Biblical Literature* 103 (1984) 599–610.

Scobie, Alex. "Slums, Sanitation, and Mortality in the Roman World." *Klio* 68 (1986) 399–433.

Scott, James C. *Domination and the Arts of Resistance: Hidden Transcripts*. New Haven: Yale University Press, 1990.

Seeley, David. *The Noble Death: Graeco-Roman Martyrology and Paul's Concept of Salvation*. Sheffield, UK: Sheffield Academic Press, 1990.

———. "Rulership and Service in Mark 10:41–45." *Novum Testamentum* 35 (1993) 234–50.

Segal, Alan. *Life after Death: A History of the Afterlife in Western Religion*. New York: Doubleday, 2004.

Shaw, Brent. "The Bandit." In *The Romans*, edited by Andrea Giardina, 300–341. Chicago: University of Chicago Press, 1993.

Shotter, David. *Nero*. 2nd ed. London: Routledge, 2005.

Szegedy-Maszak, Andrew. "Legends of the Greek Lawgivers." *Greek, Roman and Byzantine Studies* 19 (1978) 199–209.

Talbert, Charles. "Miraculous Conceptions and Births in Mediterranean Antiquity." In *The Historical Jesus in Context*, edited by Amy-Jill Levine, Dale Allison, and John Dominic Crossan, 79–86. Princeton: Princeton University Press, 2006.

Thomas, Rosalind. "Genealogy and the Genealogists." In *Greek and Roman Historiography: Oxford Readings in Classical Studies*, edited by John Marincola, 72–99. Oxford: Oxford University Press, 2011.

Toner, Jerry. *Popular Culture in Ancient Rome.* Cambridge, Polity 2009.

Tuplin, Christopher J. "The False Neros of the First Century A.D." In *Studies in Latin Literature and Roman History V*, edited by Carl Deroux, 364–404. Brussels: Latomus, 1989.

Van Henten, Jan Willem. "Noble Death and Martyrdom in Antiquity." In *Martyriumsvorstellungen in Antike und Mittelalter: Leben oder sterben für Gott?* edited by Sebastian Fuhrmann and Regina Grundmann, 85–110. Leiden: Brill, 2012.

Vermes, G. *Jesus the Jew: A Historian's Reading of the Gospels.* Philadelphia: Fortress, 1973.

Weissenrieder, Annette. "Cultural Translation: The Fig Tree and Politics of Representation under Nero in Rome (Mark 11:13–15, 19–20; Matthew 21:18–19; Luke 13:1–9). In *Miracles Revisited: New Testament Miracle Stories and Their Concepts of Reality*, edited by Stefan Alkier and Annette Weissenrieder, 201–31. Berlin: de Gruyter, 2013.

Wells, Jack. "Impiety in the Middle Republic: The Roman Response to Temple Plundering in Southern Italy. *The Classical Journal* 105 (2010) 229–43.

Williams, Craig. *Roman Homosexuality.* Oxford: Oxford University Press, 2010.

Wilson, Carol. *For I Was Hungry and You Gave Me Food: Pragmatics of Food Access in the Gospel of Matthew.* Eugene, OR: Pickwick, 2014.

Wiseman, T. P. "Legendary Genealogies in Late-Republican Rome." *Greece & Rome* 21 (1974) 153–64.

Wright, N. T. *The Resurrection of the Son of God.* Minneapolis: Fortress, 2003.

Zanker, Paul. *The Power of Images in the Age of Augustus.* Ann Arbor, MI: University of Michigan Press, 1990.

Ziolkowski, Adam. "*Urbs direpta,* or How the Romans Sacked Cities." In *War and Society in the Roman World*, edited by John Rich and Graham Shipley, 69–91. London: Routledge, 1993.

www.ingramcontent.com/pod-product-compliance
Lightning Source LLC
Chambersburg PA
CBHW020838160426
43192CB00007B/706